Mask, Fins, &

The Adventure Guide to

Maui's Best Snorkeling

Rich Schieber

Mask, Fins, & Snorkel:
The Adventure Guide to Maui's Best Snorkeling

Published by Honolua Press, LLC
P.O. Box 4581, Salem, OR 97302
www.honoluapress.com
email: info@honoluapress.com

ISBN 978-0-9898212-0-9

Printed in China

Text by Rich Schieber
Layout and Design by Sharon Schieber

All text, photography, graphics, and artwork created by Rich & Sharon Schieber unless otherwise noted. Picture of Kama'ole Beach courtesy of Dennis Zeidlhack. All underwater photography was obtained while snorkeling, not scuba diving.

For more images of the beautiful island of Maui, please visit:
senseofplacemaui.com

Safety Warning: Every effort has been made to ensure that information within this book was accurate at the time of publication. Every snorkel route described in this book has been personally snorkeled by the author. Every path described has been personally walked by the author. Every kayak route described has been personally kayaked by the author. Nonetheless, what was safe for the author may not be safe for you. Conditions change over time and entering the ocean is inherently dangerous. If you have any questions about your ability to safely complete any activity described within this book, do not attempt it. Use good judgment. Know your limits. Your safety is paramount and is your responsibility. The author and publisher assume no liability for any consequence to any party resulting from the use of this book.

I'd rather be snorkeling…

Aloha and welcome to Maui. Grab your gear, take along this guide, and I'll point you to some great snorkeling. The island of Maui has no shortage of fantastic spots and I've been lucky enough to explore them. From mellow areas perfect for beginners to challenging excursions that allow for marathon outings, Maui has it all. Whatever your comfort level, you'll discover places to remember. So get ready to have some fun, save some cash, and venture into some prime snorkeling territory.

Honolua Bay, Maui

Table of Contents

West Maui Snorkel Spots

South Maui Snorkel Spots

Kayak - Snorkeling Adventures

West Maui Excursions

South Maui Excursions

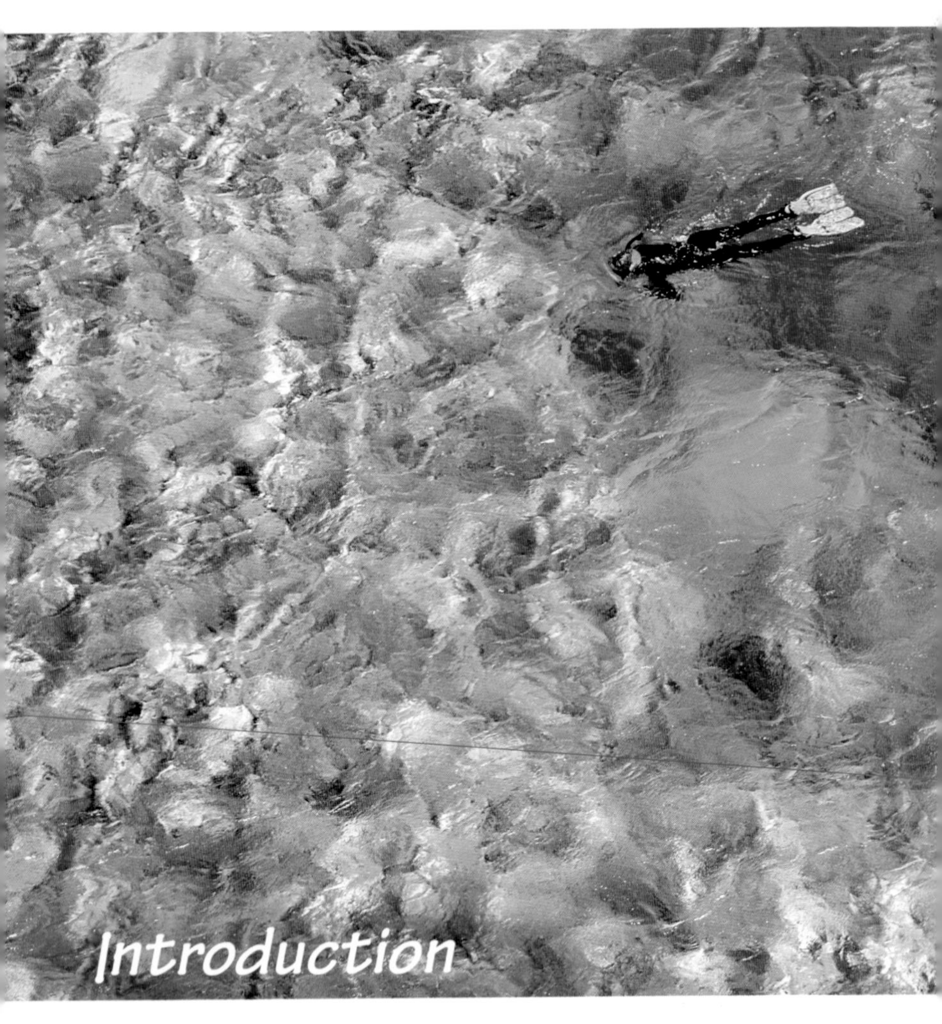

Introduction

If stranded on a desert island and provided with only three items for my survival, I'd have a difficult decision to make. Do I take food, water, and shelter, or mask, fins, and a snorkel? It's a tough call. One sustains life, the other makes life worth living—or certainly feels that way to me.

I'll admit it; I'm a snorkel fanatic. I love cruising the reef and have spent countless hours exploring Maui's waters. I've hit the sites in the free visitor magazines, and checked out places listed in travel guidebooks. I've ventured into territory mentioned on websites, and explored spots that just looked intriguing from shore. I've covered much of

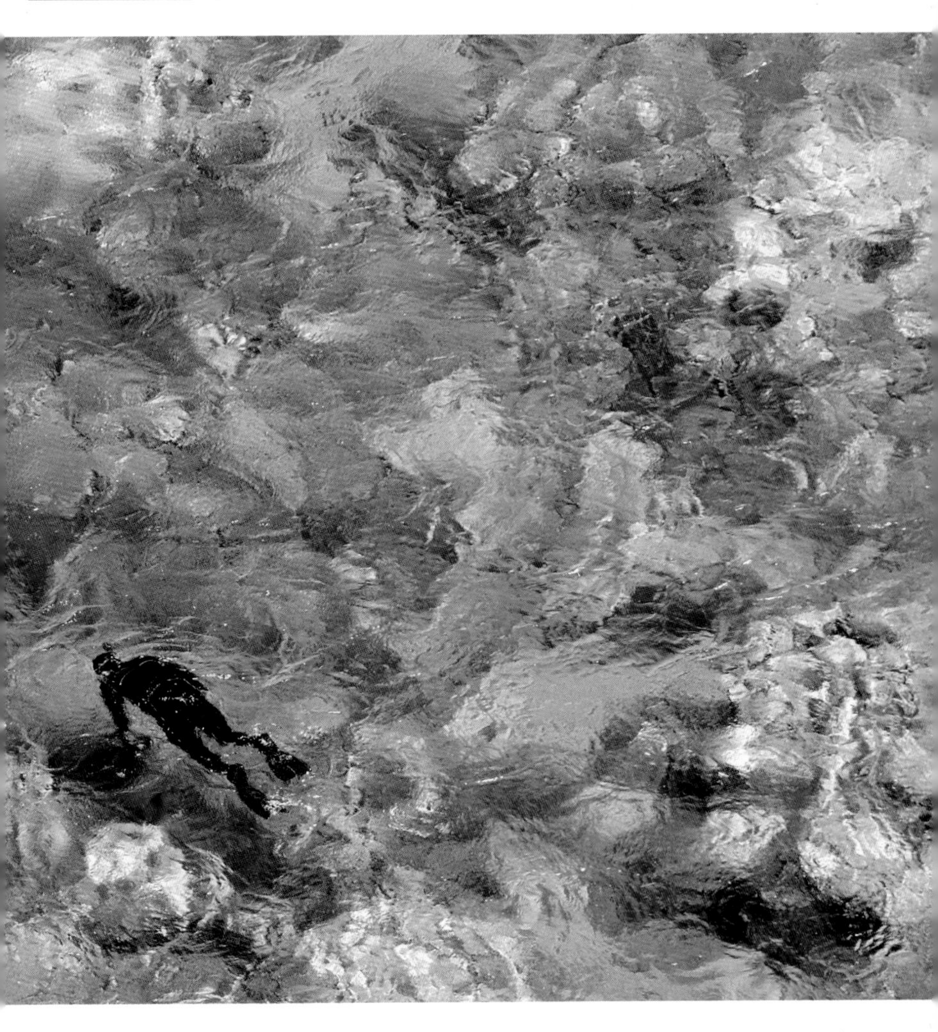

Maui's coastline and had a fantastic time learning which spots are good and which ones are great.

Every time I run into visitors looking for places to snorkel, my enthusiasm gets the best of me. I end up sharing my thoughts on various spots and suggest areas they might want to visit. It was during one of these conversations I was encouraged to write a book. I laughed it off at the time, but after hearing it again, I decided there might be something to the idea. I began taking notes following my excursions and the result is Mask, Fins, and Snorkel: The Adventure Guide to Maui's Best Snorkeling. I hope you enjoy it—Aloha!

How to use this Guide

The majority of this guide is geared toward providing you with all you need to know to explore and enjoy Maui's best snorkel spots. Each site has a complete location guide with maps, directions to get there, where to snorkel, and helpful tips specific to the spot. You'll also find advice on snorkeling, gear selection, safety, reef care, and lists of "Best Spots" depending on your interests and abilities or your location on the island. You don't need to start at the front. Read the sections that interest you most and sample others later. But do me a favor, please read the sections on Reef Care and Ocean Hazards and take the information to heart. It's important to keep yourself safe and to preserve the future of Maui's beautiful reefs.

Maui's beautiful corals and urchins

Green Sea Turtle

If you're an advanced snorkeler, the location guides and maps will get you into prime snorkeling territory quickly and easily. Reef Care, Ocean Hazards, and Snorkel Tips might also be worth a glance. If you have beginning snorkelers with you, a refresher on the basics can remind you of the essentials to share.

If you're a beginning snorkeler, the location guides and maps can help you decide where to go based on your abilities while the rest of the book will get you ready to hit the water. The Gear section will get you outfitted, and Snorkeling Basics, Reef Care, and Ocean Hazards will get you comfortable with the sport and keep you safe in the water. Once you're confident with the basics, be sure to check Snorkeling Tips to get the most out of your adventures.

For anyone snorkeling with young children, be sure to read Snorkeling with Kids. You'll find tips to make their first snorkeling experience safe, fun, and something they'll be excited to do again. Hitting any of the locations on the "Best for Kids" list will be a winner. Once you've chosen a spot, read the guide for the location and you'll be set with all the information you need for a great day at the beach.

Snorkeling

There are few things I enjoy more than slipping on my fins and heading into the water. I can easily spend hours exploring the reef and enjoying the intricate coral, colorful fish, and incredible marine life found just below the water's surface. The infinite shapes, sizes and designs are amazing. Encounters with eels, rays, and sea turtles leave me in awe. It's a beautiful and intriguing world where admission requires nothing more than a mask, fins, and snorkel. If you've never experienced the magic of the underwater world, I highly recommend snorkeling while you're on Maui. If you're already a fan, you'll love what this island has to offer. Enjoy!

Honolua Heaven!

Snorkeling Maui

Snorkeling in Maui is a little different than many other places and knowledge of those differences can make for a better excursion. Here are a couple of the most important:

Shoreline Access: This is a huge advantage! Nearly every snorkel spot on Maui can be accessed from shore. This means if you know where to go and how to get there, you have few very limits. You don't have to hop on a boat or pay anyone to take you. You're not on someone else's schedule and you have the freedom to go where you want, when you want, for as long as you want. Sometimes you'll even have the area all to yourself. And it's free. Again, this is huge! It can save you some major cash. If you've ever shelled out $75 a person to join a 100 others on a snorkel boat, you'll understand the importance quickly.

Bigfin Squid - Honolua Bay

Wind: Maui can be windy—and at times *very* windy. The wind creates waves that can make snorkeling conditions pretty lousy. Not only does it make the water choppy for swimming, but the wave action kicks up sediment creating cloudy water and low visibility—kind of a bummer for snorkeling fans. Fortunately the winds on Maui are predictable. They start to pick up in the late morning, build into midday, and can really blow by the afternoon. Thankfully it settles down in the evening.

This means your best bet for snorkeling is in the morning or earlier in the day. You'll find nicer water, safer conditions and a more enjoyable experience. But there are exceptions. The wind may not blow every day and some places may see little or none. So if you're wanting to take an afternoon snorkel, don't lose hope. Just be flexible, try a few different spots, and look for areas that receive shelter from the winds. Think Honolua Bay or Coral Gardens instead of Wailea Point or Kam I.

Snorkeling Gear

In its most basic sense, snorkeling requires nothing more than having a mask to see the sights, a snorkel to breathe, and fins to propel you through the water. It's pretty simple. It doesn't take much gear and it doesn't have to cost a lot of money. Whether you buy or rent, you can usually find a decent deal—even by Maui standards. That being said there are definite "must haves" and a few "nice to haves" to include in your gear bag. Here are tips and descriptions for each:

Must Haves

Mask: As an essential part of your gear, be sure to chose a mask that is comfortable and fits correctly. Here's how to check. Hold the mask up to your face. Does the plastic feel hard, stiff, or uncomfortable? If so, put it back and look for another. When you've found a mask that feels reasonably comfortable, inhale through your nose to create suction. A seal should develop between your face and the mask. If you hold your breath and bend forward—like taking a bow—the mask should stay put. If it does, you've got a good fit and a mask that shouldn't leak.

Anti-Fog Gel: Anti-fog gel is a serious "must have" that absolutely makes any snorkel outing better. A thin coat of gel applied to the inside of your lenses will keep them free of fog and allow you to see clearly underwater for much longer. Don't believe anyone who tells you differently or says "spit works great." Just fork over the cash for a bottle and you'll be happier. As a penny-pincher I know where to cut costs, and this isn't one of them. A small dab on each lens is all you need, so that little bottle of gel will provide several years worth of snorkeling.

If you still need convincing, here's a fact: the temperature difference between the warm air inside your mask and the cool water outside create ideal conditions for fog. As you're huffing and puffing along, you'll begin to realize you're seeing everything through a filmy haze—a major bummer for snorkelers. Think about it, the whole point is to *see* what's in the water. A little anti-fog gel will keep your mask clear for at least an hour, maybe two. My personal preference is Sea Gold Anti-Fog Gel. You can find it at most dive shops. It's been around for years.

Here's how to use it. When you arrive at your snorkel spot, grab your mask and put a pea-sized dab on the inside of each lens. Smear the gel around so the lenses are covered with a thin film. Set your mask aside while you gear-up, being careful to keep it out of the sand. When you're ready to hit the water, dip your mask in first and get the gel wet. Swirl the water around, dump it out, and proceed into the water as normal. Once you've donned your mask, if the gel seems a little thick in places, it's not a big deal. Just swirl more water inside your mask and use less gel next time. Any excess will rinse away as you snorkel and you'll soon get the hang of using it.

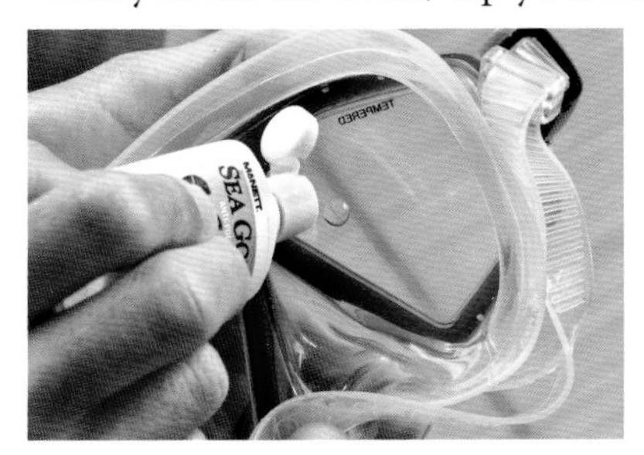

Fins: I recommend adjustable strap fins. They're simple, straightforward, and get the job done. Some people use scuba fins that fit over reef shoes or booties, but they can be heavy and cumbersome. I own an expensive, high-end pair of diving fins, but prefer my low-priced "kit" fins for snorkeling. They give plenty of thrust per kick and don't weigh a ton hiking to the beach. The additional length of scuba fins can also make them harder to maneuver, particularly in shallow areas. Taking care around coral is important, you don't want to bump or kick it with your fins.

On the other extreme I often see people snorkeling without fins. Certainly there's no rule that says you have to use fins, but I wouldn't consider snorkeling without them. If you plan on covering any distance, fins make swimming easier—particularly if you're up against any current. Their efficiency in propelling you forward lets you enjoy the wonders around you instead exerting yourself getting from point A to point B. Fins also offer a safety advantage as ocean conditions and circumstances can change unexpectedly. Having the ability to propel yourself quickly to shore is a significant safety benefit. Not to mention, fins are just fun. The more you snorkel and develop your technique, the sooner you'll understand how turtles and fish can be incredibly fast and amazingly gracefully all at the same time.

Snorkel: Most snorkels available today have decent purge valves, splash guards, and flexible, comfortable mouthpieces. If the snorkel you're considering doesn't have these features or you're unsure, ask a clerk and be sure to get one that does. The splash guard at the top of the snorkel does just what it sounds like and is especially useful when waves are kicking up. The purge valve at the other end makes it easy to expel any water that gets past the splash guard. A flexible, comfortable mouthpiece feels better and goes unnoticed, while a poorly fitting one can be so annoying it distracts from the sights. Thankfully, you don't have to spend a mint for a good snorkel. My inexpensive "kit" snorkel works just as well as a $50 one. I own both, tried them back-to-back, and wish I'd saved the fifty bucks!

Flotation Device: If your swimming ability isn't the best or you're the least bit uncomfortable in water, a flotation device is a "must have." Your enjoyment and safety will increase dramatically. Panic is the enemy of anyone not confident in the water. Even wearing snorkel gear, it's easy for inexperienced swimmers to give in to irrational fears and begin having problems—particularly if ocean conditions become rougher than when they started. A flotation device can also be gentler on the coral. The extra buoyancy provides confidence and maneuverability in tight or shallow spots. I've witnessed far too many people kicking and damaging coral while trying to maintain control in the water. It's much better to be safe, confident, and in control from the start.

Flotation devices come in many varieties ranging from foam noodles to snorkel vests or belts. For some, a foam noodle held under the arms and across the chest is enough to put them at ease. My wife prefers wearing a neoprene water ski vest. She began snorkeling before learning to swim and appreciated the confidence it provided. Unlike a noodle, a vest doesn't get in the way, stays-put, and requires no other thought once it's on. They're pricey and take up some luggage space, but for safety and peace of mind it's worth it to us. Even after learning to swim, my wife still likes wearing her vest. It makes maneuvering a breeze and is a great reassurance on long outings or in rough conditions.

Nice to Have

Neoprene Strap Cover: A strap cover for your mask makes putting it on and taking it off easier and more comfortable. Particularly with long hair, a neoprene cover allows a mask to be slipped on or slid off without wrestling a rubber strap through wet hair. The cover consist of two pieces of neoprene sewn together on one side with Velcro attached on the other. The neoprene slides over the mask straps and is secured by Velcro. In any case, they're great. Certainly not a "have to have," but they make things easier. Just make sure the scratchy side of the Velcro is turned away from your neck—lesson learned the hard way!

Shorty Wet Suit: Whenever I snorkel, I'm usually in the water for hours at a time. Even in the warmth of tropical waters, I always get cold. Whether you're prone to cold or want to snorkel at length, a shorty makes eventual temperature loss more manageable. If you tend to get chilly, definitely consider one. Made out of neoprene, a shorty can also protect you from the sun, jellyfish, and mild abrasions from lava rocks.

Reef Shoes: When I refer to reef shoes, I don't mean anything elaborate, just something lightweight to protect your feet. I use the slip-on style that have rubber soles and stretch fabric across the top. You can find cheap reef shoes at any variety store on Maui. They're nothing fancy, but you'll definitely appreciate them when you're trekking across a rocky path or lava shoreline.

Nylon Net Bag: Some snorkel kits come with a travel bag made of nylon netting. They're not particularly comfortable for carrying gear. I prefer using a canvas shoulder-style snorkel bag instead. But don't toss out the net bag if you get one. They're great for taking your reef shoes with you while you're snorkeling. This is helpful if you want to enter the water at one location, exit somewhere else, and walk back afterwards. When I'm entering the water from rough terrain, I wear my reef shoes in, then slip them into the net bag after switching to my fins. I keep a small piece of foam in the bag for buoyancy (cut from a foam noodle) and secure the bag at my waist.

Buying or Renting Gear

When it comes to equipment, there are lots of options on Maui. Dozens of businesses sell and/or rent snorkeling gear. Take advantage of the abundance of shops to check out your gear options. Try on masks, ask questions, and price daily and weekly rental rates. You'll find many shops are quite reasonable. Some resorts also rent equipment right on the beach, but plan on spending more.

Try to decide if it makes more sense for you to buy or rent. If you plan to snorkel a lot, owning your equipment will soon pay for itself and you'll appreciate having your own gear. The flip side is traveling with it. Do you have room in your bags? Will the airlines charge a higher fee for the extra weight? The right choice might be something in-between—buying gear for the most avid snorkelers in your group, while renting for the rest.

I bought a US Divers snorkel kit at Costco on my second day in Maui. It was reasonably priced and worked extremely well. Eventually I upgraded my mask, but still use the fins and snorkel from the kit. For as much as we enjoy snorkeling, we always travel with our own gear and appreciate the flexibility it provides.

Honolua Bay is a great spot to bring your reef shoes.

Ocean Hazards

Anytime you enter the ocean there are hazards. Knowing what they are and how to manage them can reduce your risk. Be smart, play it safe, and use good judgment. Also recognize the single biggest danger while swimming in Maui is drowning. While not as sensational as a shark encounter, drowning claims many more lives. So before you enter the water, be honest with yourself about your abilities. If you're not the best swimmer, use a flotation device or don't venture far from shore. It's also a wise practice to never snorkel alone.

Breaking waves near White Rock

Surf: Breaking waves can be beautiful to look at, but unless you're on a boogie board trying to catch one, it's best to steer clear of the surf zone while snorkeling. When entering or exiting the water, move through it quickly. Pay attention to what's going on and don't dawdle. A breaking wave can level you in an instant and tends to take the fun out of the day.

A good habit to develop before entering or exiting the water is to spend a few minutes watching the waves. Take note of where the waves are breaking, their size, and timing. If you watch the ocean enough, you'll begin to notice that waves tend to arrive in sets—a series of waves that come through one after another. Sets tend to vary. Sometimes a set will have several similarly sized waves followed by a few larger ones.

Other times the new set can be much larger than the last. Between sets there is usually a period of calm water before the process begins again. Use this understanding to time your movement through the break zone and keep yourself safe. If you arrive at a spot with heavy surf, toss the idea of snorkeling altogether. There's no point in taking a risk. It's not only dangerous, but rough surf kicks up sand and makes water clarity lousy.

Surge: Surge is the upward rhythmic movement of the water as waves make their way toward shore. Before snorkeling around rocky shores or outcroppings, keep in mind the degree of force that passing waves and surge are generating. It's pretty obvious if the waves are slamming the rocks, it's best to keep your distance. But even when waves aren't packing a punch, incoming surge can push you into unintended spots. Just like waves, surge can also pick up and become stronger. If you're investigating a tight area try to anticipate the surge—it's very rhythmic. Before the surge reaches you, turn around so your head faces the force and use your fins to control your movement. You'll find you can maintain your position quite well. Practice this technique in open areas and you'll soon get it down. It's a great skill to have and can keep you out of a jam.

Before snorkeling in shallow reef areas, take into account the changing water level each wave brings with it. Keep in mind the degree of

Keep alert - surge and ocean conditions can change quickly.

change will determine whether you can safely swim over a coral head or rocky area. High and low tide can also play into access of shallow areas. Sometimes a spot that is too shallow during low tide can be completely accessible at another time. Rule of thumb, if an area appears too shallow, avoid it. Take it from me, being slammed against lava rock by surge is not a pleasant experience.

Rip Currents: Rip currents are the number one danger at the beach, but they don't have to be. If you understand their nature and what to do if you get caught in one, you can manage the situation and return to shore or await rescue.

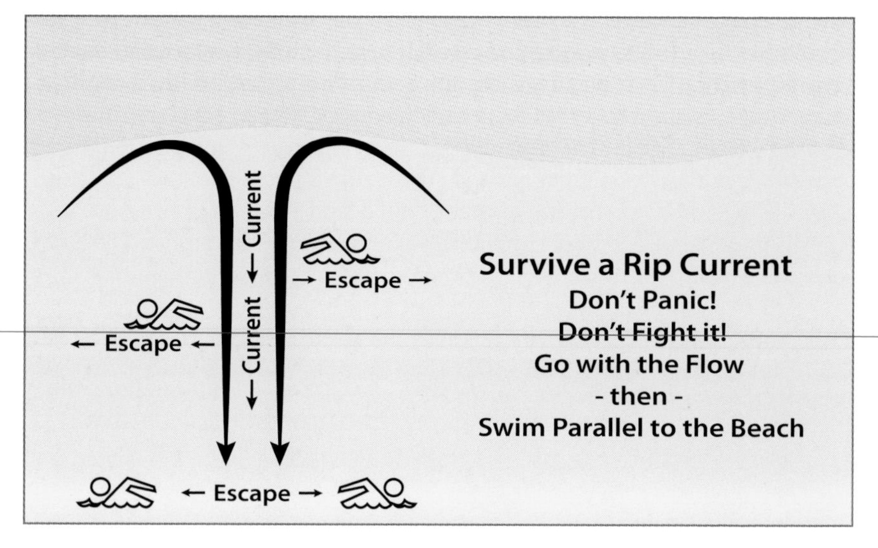

A rip current is a powerful channel of water that flows swiftly from the beach out toward sea. They usually develop along low spots of the shoreline. Instead of a wave simply receding like it does on a flat or protected beach, water naturally flows toward this low point. As water accumulates it gains speed and force and upon reaching the low spot it funnels into a channel as it flows back out to sea. Fortunately, rip currents tend to be fairly narrow and dissipate as they move away from shore. If you're ever caught in a rip current remember:

Don't Panic and Don't Fight It!

Recognize a rip for what it is and "go with the flow" and/or swim parallel along the beach to get yourself out of the current. Remember as a rip current moves away from the beach it will dissipate and you can escape it. Most rips usually diminish within a few hundred feet. The flow of a rip can be powerful and trying to swim against it can lead to panic and exhaustion. Instead, save your energy, keep your wits about you, and know that your fins provide a major safety advantage. If you stay calm and think logically you will have no problem returning to shore.

Sunburn: The sun can be fierce on Maui and if you don't take precautions, you'll pay the price. It's particularly easy for a sunburn to sneak up on you when you're snorkeling. To guard against it, many people wear T-shirts or "skins" to keep their backs covered and use sunscreen to protect other exposed areas. Whenever you're hitting the water, it's a smart practice to apply sunscreen at least 20 minutes beforehand. The extra time is believed to increase its effectiveness and diminish the negative impact it has on coral. Better yet, consider using an eco-friendly sunscreen and wear sun protective clothing when you can.

Jellyfish: Knock on wood, I have yet to be stung by a jellyfish—and I'd like to keep it that way! Thankfully Maui doesn't have quite the problem found in Oahu's waters, but reports of stings do occur. I was present when someone tangled with a Portuguese Man of War on Lana'i. It was painful just to watch. If you're in the water and see jellyfish, get to shore. If you hear reports of them being in the water, don't go in. If you're stung, vinegar can help lessen the sting. Seek medical help if needed.

A researcher in Oahu has determined that the Hawaiian Box Jellyfish tends to make an appearance 8-10 days after a full moon. Others suggest 7-12 days. I tend to limit my water activities from day 7 through day 10 following a full moon.

Urchins: Maui has several great snorkel locations where the unobservant runs the risk of an urchin spine in the foot or hand. It's not a pleasant prospect. You can avoid the experience by being particularly alert when entering or exiting the water, or swimming through shallow rocky areas. While these spiny creatures add to the scenery, their sharp probes can puncture the skin, break off, and exact pain for days. Vinegar is a commonly recommended treatment, but it doesn't completely eliminate the pain—it's best to avoid contact in the first place.

Banded Urchin

Coral: Touching coral can leave you with a nasty cut that's remarkably slow to heal. It can also damage or kill the coral. Take great care in shallow areas and tight spots to avoid being pushed into it by unexpected surge. Coral can also host numerous marine bacteria and toxins. In the event you get cut while snorkeling, thoroughly clean the area as soon as possible to avoid infection.

Lionfish: Beautiful to look at—ugly to touch. These fish and their friend the Scorpionfish, have needle-like spines that carry powerful venom for those who get too close. As a snorkeler you likely won't encounter a Red Lionfish, but you may come across the less elaborate Green Lionfish or a Scorpionfish. They tend to crouch on coral and blend in extremely well. Their disguised presence is yet another reason to keep your hands to yourself while snorkeling! In the unlikely event you get envenomated, it's recommended to soak the injury in hot water for 30-90 minutes. Studies show this kills the venom and reduces the severity of the sting. As always, seek medical attention if needed.

Sharks: Statistically speaking, the chances of being attacked by a shark are extremely low. In fact, it's highly unlikely you'll even see one. But that doesn't mean sharks aren't around—they are present throughout the waters of Hawaii. Thankfully the majority of sharks encountered in shallower reef and snorkel areas are Whitetip Reef Sharks. Occasionally found resting under ledges, Whitetips are not harmless by any means, but they're also not "man-eaters." So if you're fortunate enough to come upon one, treasure the sighting and leave your fear at home. Just give them plenty of space and enjoy their presence from a distance.

Tiger Sharks are a different story altogether. These guys can be very dangerous. Fortunately, snorkelers rarely make their acquaintance. However it can happen. While extremely rare, Tiger Sharks are believed to be implicated in at least 9 injury incidents with snorkelers and swimmers on Maui from 2000 to 2013. If you add non-tigers and non-identified sharks to the mix, the total rises to at least 15. Sure, it's a scary thought, but if you consider the number of visitors during this span—over 30 million—you get a little perspective. The reality is that the chance of a Tiger Shark attack is incredibly low.

There are many avoidance strategies meant to reduce the possibility of a shark encounter, but recognize that as long as you are swimming in the ocean there are no guarantees. Here's a list of the most commonly suggested avoidance tactics:

- Avoid swimming in murky water—snorkeling in these conditions is no fun anyway.
- Avoid snorkeling in low light conditions such as dawn or dusk when sharks tend to feed. It's important to note however, that many attacks in Hawaii have taken place in bright sunny conditions and clear water.
- Avoid being in areas with blood in the water. If you see a lot of spear fishing going on it's best to move on. Avoid docks or other heavy fishing areas.
- Always snorkel with at least one other person. The presence of a group is thought to reduce the chance of an attack.
- Avoid snorkeling near the mouth of a stream or river, or over a sudden drop-off into deep water. Sharks like hunting in both of these areas.

Reef Care

It's a sad fact, but the world's coral reefs are struggling to survive. Climate change, increased ocean acidity, over-fishing, hazardous run-off, and pollution are all taking their toll. Unfortunately, Maui's reefs are not immune. Careless human interaction is also at fault. Please learn and practice good snorkeling behaviors and encourage others to do the same. Here are a few things to keep in mind.

Don't Touch the Coral: Every time a person touches coral, it can weaken and die. Whether it's an intentional reaching out and wanting to feel the coral or a careless kick of a fin, it has the same effect. While some rationalize, "it's just a little touch," each "little touch" adds up. Multiply it by several thousand snorkelers a year and you get the idea. Regrettably, examples can be seen in many places around the island.

Watch your Fins: It's easy to forget, but fins add length to your legs. Depending on the style, this can range from 18 inches to well over 2 feet. Make sure you account for this extra length, particularly when you're stopped in an upright position to take a break, adjust your mask, or converse with your snorkeling companions. Too many times I've seen snorkelers tread water as they talk, while their fins slap the coral below. An effective technique used by experienced snorkelers is to raise your knees as if you're sitting. It keeps your fins higher in the water and further away from the coral. You'll find the salt water and your swimming ability will keep you buoyant without much need to tread water. If you're unable to do this comfortably, you need a flotation device.

Skip the Fish Food: A once popular practice that's fortunately going by the way side is feeding fish while snorkeling or diving. It may sound like fun: pull out a piece of food and watch the fish swarm around you. The problem is that this short-term thrill has long lasting impact. It dramatically changes the reef dynamics and fish variety by encouraging aggressive fish and feeding behavior while pushing out other fish. An example of this is when you enter an area that's seen heavy fish feeding and are approached by a bunch of Sergeants looking for a hand-out. The initial "cuteness" is quickly lost once you begin to notice a quantifiable lack of any other fish.

Please, please, please don't stand on coral heads!

Use Smart Sunscreen Practices: Apply sunscreen at least 20 minutes before entering the water. By giving sunscreen time to absorb it protects your skin better and less will wash off into the water. An estimated 4-6000 metric tons of sunscreen washes off swimmers' bodies annually with serious potential to damage fragile reefs. Consider using "eco-friendly" sunscreens and sun-protective clothing.

Snorkeling Basics

Entering the Water: When you're ready to hit the water always take time to watch the waves first. Take note of where they're breaking, their size, and timing to guide your movement through the break zone. Getting in is pretty simple. I carry my fins in one hand, my mask and snorkel in the other, and wade in past the breakers. As I'm moving through the water I scan the bottom for potential toe-breakers and dip my mask to get some rinsing action on the anti-fog gel. I always move pretty quickly. Once past the breakers, I float on my back in a modified sitting position, slip on my mask, pull on my fins, and head out.

Quite often I've watched snorkelers enter the water in a backwards march with their fins already on their feet. It's a technique divers use, but I'd advise against it when snorkeling. It's incredibly clumsy, and without a heavy tank on your back, there's really no need. It also slows your progress getting through the break zone and it's never wise to turn your back on the ocean.

Poʻolenalena Beach

Exiting the Water: Exiting is pretty much the same steps in reverse. I take a moment to see what the ocean is doing, watch for snorkelers, rocks and urchins, and make my way forward. I tend to keep my mask and fins on for as long as I can to take advantage of the benefits of both. Before things get too shallow I remove my fins, stand up, and quickly move through the break zone—pretty easy.

Ornate Butterflyfish

Clearing your Mask: If you pick a mask with a good fit, the occasions of getting water inside will be limited. But from time to time it happens. Thankfully, eliminating water from your mask is easy. You don't need to remove your mask or even take a break from snorkeling. Here's what to do: while keeping your mask underwater, tilt your head back and gently apply pressure to the upper portion of your mask. Exhale through your nose. This will cause the water to drain out the bottom of your mask. It's a simple trick and works great with a little practice.

Clearing your Snorkel: Most snorkels today are designed with a splashguard to help keep water from getting into the breathing tube. They work well, but if you dive below the surface to see something, you're going to wind up with water in your snorkel. It just goes with the territory and is really no big deal. To clear it, exhale forcefully when you return to the surface. The water will be expelled and you can continue breathing through your snorkel as before. Practice with a few shallow dives and you'll quickly get the hang of it.

Where to Snorkel: While the majority of this book provides extensive details on specific locations, if you're new to the activity it's worthwhile to mention what factors contribute to a good snorkel spot. Assuming that you're most interested in seeing marine life there are predictable areas to look. As a general rule the rocks and coral that create the reef provide food and shelter for many of the creatures in the ocean and as such offer the best opportunity for snorkeling. On many of South Maui's long sandy beaches reefs are often found at each end where rocky points extend into the ocean and provide places for coral to grow. If you arrive at an unfamiliar area and wonder what's below the surface you're likely to have more luck—and a shorter swim—if you begin snorkeling closer to the rocky ends of the beach than from the middle of the sand. A long sandy beach can often

have a featureless underwater landscape a bit like a sand desert, while rock formations offer coral teeming with life and activity. But like everything, there can be exceptions. Several of West Maui beaches have reefs directly out from the sand.

When to Snorkel: Certain weather and ocean conditions are much more conducive to snorkeling than others. If it's your first time snorkeling and you arrive to whipping winds and rough waves at the beach, leave it for another day. Splashing waves and surge can make it tough going, kick up a ton of sand in the water, and greatly reduce what you can see. It's nothing like snorkeling on a calm day! Sunshine makes a difference too. If the sky is overcast or thick clouds block the sun, you won't see as vibrant of colors or enjoy the same clarity as snorkeling on a clear day. That's not to say it won't be fun, but the difference can be like turning on a bright light in a dark closet.

Pu'u Ola'i from Wailea Point

Cleaning your Gear: Following each outing, it's important to rinse your gear with fresh water. The salt in the ocean can be pretty rough on things. Developing a gear rinsing habit will help your equipment last longer and have it ready to go for the next outing. It's also a good practice to occasionally clean the lenses of your mask. A little toothpaste and tap water on each lens will get them back into shape in minutes.

Snorkeling Tips

Every snorkeler I've encountered enjoys seeing fish and they all share the desire to see even more. Here are a few tips to better your chances and advance your skills.

Keep your Hands at your Sides: If you want to see fish, splashing through an area like an Olympic swimmer isn't the way to do it. It'll scare them away. Instead keep your hands at your sides and propel yourself with your fins. It's a trick scuba divers learn in training and it works well to keep from chasing off the creatures you're out to see. Try it for a while and you'll realize you have all the power you need right at your feet.

Quiet your Fins: Next time you're snorkeling, pay attention to the noise you're making. If your fins are slapping or chopping through the water, take a few minutes to work on your technique. Fins actually work better by using the full length of your legs to kick. It's your hips and thighs doing most of the work, not your knees. Concentrate on letting the power of your kick come from your hips rather than your knees. Just a few tweaks in your style will propel you more quietly and efficiently through the water—with fewer charley horses in your calves!

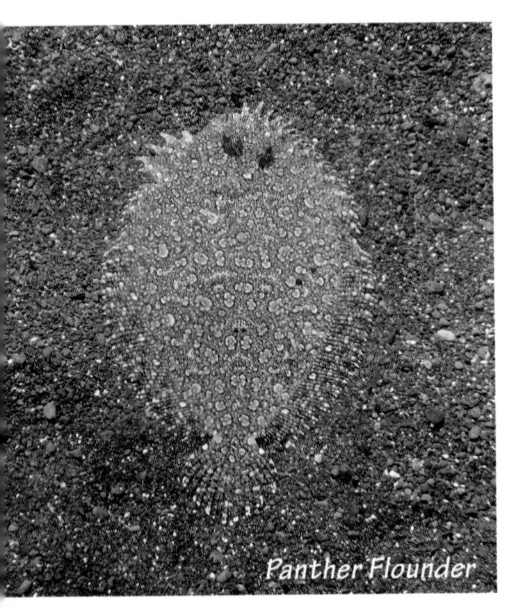

Panther Flounder

Take it Slow: A popular Maui bumper sticker reads: Slow Down—This ain't the Mainland. It's a sentiment that's equally applicable while snorkeling. When you enter the water and slip on your mask, think island time and take it slow. Many of the most interesting sea creatures are experts at camouflage. When you slow your pace, you'll pick up details that are easy to miss and you'll see more reef life than ever before. Many times I've watched snorkelers cruise right past an octopus. If they hadn't been in such a rush, they would have seen it.

Juvenile Whitemouth Moray Eel

Think Small: It's easy to be enthralled by a huge Blue Trevally, but if you look closely at some of the smaller creatures of the reef, you will find equally engaging traits. A dive instructor once told me he enjoyed large fish, but it was the tiniest that really captured his attention. The intricate colors and details on something so small thoroughly fascinated him. I think he was on to something.

Once while snorkeling all over a bay hoping to discover its every creature, I noticed my wife seemed glued to one spot. Later I discovered she had a front row seat to numerous juvenile fish species in nurseries along the rocky edges of the shore. She was mesmerized by hundreds of tiny colorful fish going about their day just in front of her mask. Take time to observe the smallest of creatures and you'll add a whole new dimension to your snorkeling experience.

Snorkeling with Kids

One evening at Ekahi Village Condos, I noticed a father and his young son snorkeling at the pool. What captured my attention was the quality of their interaction. The boy's father was not only helping his son to become comfortable with his equipment, but teaching him hand signals so they could communicate non-verbally underwater. Along with the standard "okay" sign, and the shivering "I'm cold" sign, they were creating signals to indicate what types of creatures they were hoping to see. The enjoyment and engagement of both father and son was readily apparent. Their pool time was not only a fun and practical way to practice snorkeling, but created a treasured memory I'm sure the son will have for the rest of his life. Who knows? Maybe I was witnessing the early education of the next Jacques Cousteau. Then again, maybe the next Cousteau resides in your family. By getting kids comfortable in the pool and confident with their gear you can jump-start their interest and increase the likelihood of having a great "first snorkel" when you're ready to hit the reef.

Gear: Getting children familiar with their gear starts outside the water. Let them try on their equipment and see what it's like to breathe through the snorkel and see things through their mask. Take a moment to make basic mask adjustments if needed. Explain each piece of equipment and its function keeping it simple and fun. You can make the introduction to their gear as imaginative or as straight forward as you want, using whatever method works best to engage your kids. If you want to get creative, young children will develop a better understanding of their gear by making comparisons they can grasp and enjoy—fins are like having duck feet, or blowing water out the top of the snorkel is like a spouting whale.

Pool Practice: The next step is practicing in a swimming pool, with the shallow end being the place to start. Initially you'll want to skip the fins and experiment with just the snorkel and mask. The goal is to get your child comfortable wearing the mask and breathing through the mouth piece and snorkel. Most kids will probably handle their first time in the water with equipment just fine as long as you keep it fun and take things at a pace that is comfortable for them.

It's easier to experiment wearing both the mask and snorkel in the pool, but if your child is hesitant or feels claustrophobic wearing both, you may want to back up and take things a step at a time. Let your child get accustomed to the mask and snorkel separately before wearing both, keeping things simple, light-hearted, and fun. Particularly with a more apprehensive child, your goal is to build confidence by focusing on the positives and developing trust in his or her gear. For bolder kids, putting on their mask and snorkel and letting them play may be all the introduction they need. Once your child is comfortable with both, add fins to the mix and they'll quickly discover the new found power of swimming with finned feet.

There are lots of things you can practice together in the pool—from developing non-verbal communication, to using your fins to maneuver. With a little experimenting, kids will get the hang of how their fins can help them to turn, back up, or stay in one place. Children can also learn how to clear water out of their mask, check the "Snorkel Basics" section for the steps (p.23). Retrieving coins or other items from the bottom of the pool is made easy with a mask and snorkel and offers a great way to practice diving below the surface and clearing water from the snorkel. Tell them to exhale forcefully through the snorkel when they surface, and they'll be spouting just like the whales around Maui.

Once kids become comfortable in the pool and confident with their gear, they're ready for the reef. Prior to arriving at the beach—before excitement has reached its peak—take a few moments to clearly explain your expectations for safety and communication, then go have fun!

Flotation Devices: A beginning snorkeler with *any* swimming concerns should *always* use a flotation device. It's safe and will increase snorkeling enjoyment by boosting confidence and alleviating fear. Panic is the enemy of anyone not confident in the water. Even wearing snorkel gear, it's easy for an inexperienced swimmer to give in to irrational fears and begin having problems. Using a flotation device helps puts those fears to rest. A simple foam "noodle" held under the arms and across the chest can often be enough to put someone at ease. A flotation belt or life vest can be even better. A life jacket requires little thought or hassle once you've put it on. You don't have to hang onto it or keep track of it and it can't get pulled away should ocean conditions change.

For non-swimmers, be sure to allow time for them to develop trust and confidence in their flotation device. With a little time and reassurance, they'll soon enjoy snorkeling as much as you.

Buddy System: Stick together and use the buddy system. Not only does this provide a sense of safety, the joy of discovery is increased by having someone to share it with. Holding hands makes it easy to stay close together if your child will allow it. Often a quick squeeze is all it takes to direct someone's attention before they miss seeing that "cool fish" swim by or the eel that just poked its head from the rocks.

Take Pictures: An underwater camera on a snorkel trip is a tremendous amount of fun. For older kids, it provides an additional dimension to snorkeling, or can help distract a new snorkeler who may be feeling a bit anxious. Pictures also provide a great way to share the experience with others and identify the creatures you've seen. There are many reasonably priced underwater cameras available, even cheap disposables, though I'd recommend spending more and going digital. A digital allows you to enjoy your images immediately, share them with friends, and take as many pictures as you want. If you didn't bring an underwater camera with you, the Costco in Kahului is always a good bet.

Books: Most kids are curious and get a great deal of satisfaction being able to identify the sea life they encounter. You can take their snorkeling experience to the next level by picking up a basic identification book

Blackside Hawkfish like to perch on coral.

for the marine life in Hawaii. It can be a great resource for learning the names of sea creatures and just may inspire a budding oceanographer in your family.

Underwater Photography

It may sound crazy, but I once spent over an hour trying to get the perfect shot of an octopus. If the waves hadn't started pounding, I likely would have been at it longer. I'll admit it was a bit obsessive, but once you start taking underwater pictures, you'll understand. Underwater photography is a lot of fun, but if you're trying to get something better than a blurry snapshot it can also be extremely challenging. When I was finished with my "octopus shoot," I had shot over 200 pictures and only 3 were keepers. Thankfully, it's not usually that difficult! Here are a few tips that can increase your chances of getting a good shot.

Day Octopus at Ulua Reef.

Timing: Get to know your camera. Take a lot of shots and pay attention to how your camera responds. The single biggest problem with point-and-shoot cameras and underwater photography is the lag-time between the moment you press the shutter and the time it takes for the camera to take the picture and record it. It may surprise you, but it's not instantaneous, and some cameras are worse than others. The result is a lot of missed shots and blurry images.

Shutter-lag issues become apparent when a cool fish zips by and you scramble to get the shot. You press the shutter release and seconds later the only thing in the preview is a fish tail—bummer! To minimize this issue, try to anticipate the movement of your subject. If a fish is swimming in a certain direction, consider where it might be by the time your camera actually snaps the pic and frame your shot accordingly. If you're diving down to take a picture of an eel, pay attention to your own movement through the water. After you descend, your body's natural buoyancy will pull you back to the surface. Account for it and take your shot quickly before you start floating away from the eel.

You may also be able to make shooting adjustments to your camera—a good reason to read the manual and experiment. Many cameras will allow you to change settings or use different modes to account for a variety of conditions. You may find shooting in "sports mode" results in fewer blurry shots as this setting increases shutter speed to stop the action of moving objects. You may also want to consider a faster SD card. A higher-end SD card can often process faster and store more pictures than the standard card typically included with a new camera.

Conditions: Wind, waves, surge, and current can all add to the difficulty in capturing the shot you want. The problem rests with the constant movement of the water. Either you're pushed out of position and miss your subject or you're jostled at the moment you press the shutter release and get a blurry picture. By recognizing which conditions are presenting the challenges you can sometimes work around them. If it's really choppy, dive underwater or time your shots to occur between waves. If the current or surge is pushing you out of position, try approaching your subject from a different angle.

Lighting: It's important to realize that as you descend deeper into the water, your pictures will lose color. It's evident in the blue cast you'll notice when you compare your underwater pictures to those taken above the surface. This is because water filters the colors of the light spectrum, causing them to gradually fade from view. At about 10 feet, some colors completely disappear. The deeper you descend, the more the various colors are filtered. Eventually all colors slowly fade until you're in complete darkness. Interestingly enough, the warmest colors of the light spectrum fade first, with red absent at about 10 feet, followed by orange at 25 feet, and yellow around 35. Fortunately, color loss is a minimal issue for snorkelers because you're mostly swimming near the surface. If it's a bright, sunny day the only change in color you may notice are in red or

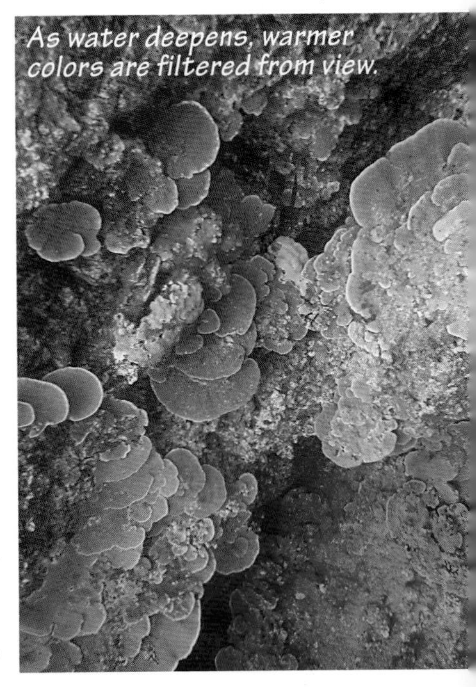

As water deepens, warmer colors are filtered from view.

Taken in shallow water...

orange hues. On the other hand, divers usually need additional light to take pictures or their images will be devoid of most colors other than shades of blue.

The easiest way to get bright colorful images is by taking your pictures in shallower water. The abundance of natural bright light will keep colors vivid and reduce shadowy areas in your image. You can experiment with your camera's built-in flash, but just like sunlight from above, light from your flash will dissipate as it's filtered by the water. Your subject needs to be close or the flash won't help. Additionally if conditions are rough and there's a lot of sand in the water, the light from your flash can reflect off the particles closest to your camera giving your picture a grainy appearance. Experiment a little and you'll figure out what works best for the conditions you're in. If you want to get technical (and spend money) there are lights made specifically for underwater photography, as well as software programs to restore faded or missing colors. If you're in the market for an underwater camera or housing be sure to check diving websites for reviews. In particular, look for cameras that perform well in low light to reduce the amount of "noise" in your images—a hassle inherent to underwater photography.

...these butterflyfish are brightly colored.

Fill Your SD Card: I've shot literally thousands of pictures while snorkeling in Maui. I live by the adage of "more is better" and shoot, and shoot, and shoot! I'd rather toss out a couple hundred images and end up with a few of great shots, than take ten pictures and come away with nothing. Thanks to the advancements of digital photography, there's no downside to shooting multiple pictures except running out of battery power or space on your card. So don't hesitate to take multiple shots, I guarantee you'll dramatically increase your number of keepers. And you just might discover how enjoyable it is to spend an hour hanging with an octopus.

Editing programs can help brighten images taken in deeper water.

Fish Pictured:
Top left - Fourspot Butterflyfish
Bottom left - Oval Butterflyfish
Above - Spotted Boxfish

Skip the Spearfishing

If you've thought about spearfishing while visiting Maui, I have a huge favor to ask. Please reconsider your plans and skip the spearfishing. Here's why:

I've been snorkeling Maui's reefs for many years and have noticed a disturbing trend. Large fish that were once plentiful are becoming harder to find, their numbers having dropped considerably. One constant during this decline has been the explosive growth in the number of visitors spearfishing. It's truly striking. Not long ago, it was uncommon to see a snorkeler carrying a spear, today it's rare not to see one. While I've debated the issue with a number of local spear-fishermen, it doesn't take a genius to see a connection. More tourists spearfishing means fewer large fish inhabiting the reefs. It's that simple.

Helping to solve the problem is pretty simple too. Just skip it. If you're dying for a fish dinner, order fish at a restaurant or stop by a fish market. Fresh fish is available everywhere on Maui and the vendors will appreciate your business. If you're yearning to match wits with a

Bluespotted Cornetfish

fish, recognize that spearing a fish isn't particularly challenging. A much tougher challenge is "shooting" a fish with your underwater camera and coming away with a fantastic shot.

This snorkeling guide can put you into some awesome spots, please don't ruin them by wiping out the fish. Skip the spearfishing. Be a part of the solution, not the problem. Then if you're lucky enough to encounter a giant parrotfish or a huge Bluefin Trevally, recognize the beauty of the moment and realize it wouldn't have happened had someone arrived earlier with a spear.

Location Guides

You may notice that the location guides included in this book are all in West Maui and South Maui. There's a reason. I visited Maui for many years before moving here and after countless hours of exploring the waters, it's where I consistently found the best snorkeling. That's not to say there aren't other great spots. Hana, Ke'anae, and the far northern points of West Maui offer some enticing areas, but the challenges presented by isolation and unpredictable conditions keep them from being ranked as the "Best." Too many of my Hana snorkel excursions were derailed by rough seas. Sure, the beautiful views and banana bread can take the bite out of three hours of endless corners, but if your main goal is snorkeling, stick to the west and south sides of the island. They're by far your best bet for consistently good snorkeling.

South Maui

Kama'ole I
Keawakapu Beach
Ulua Beach
Wailea Beach
Polo Beach
Palauea Beach
Po'olenalena Beach
Chang's Beach
Five Caves - Five Graves
Makena Landing
Maluaka Beach
Little Beach
Ahihi Cove
Ahihi Bay
La Pérouse

West Maui

Honolua Bay
Mokule'ia Bay
Namalu Bay
Kapalua Bay
Napili Bay
Kahekili Beach
Black Rock
Olowalu MM14
Coral Gardens

Kayak Snorkel Excursions

Makena Landing to Pu'u Ola'i
Makena Landing to White Rock
Makena Landing Highlights
Olowalu
Pali "Cliffs"

Map Legend

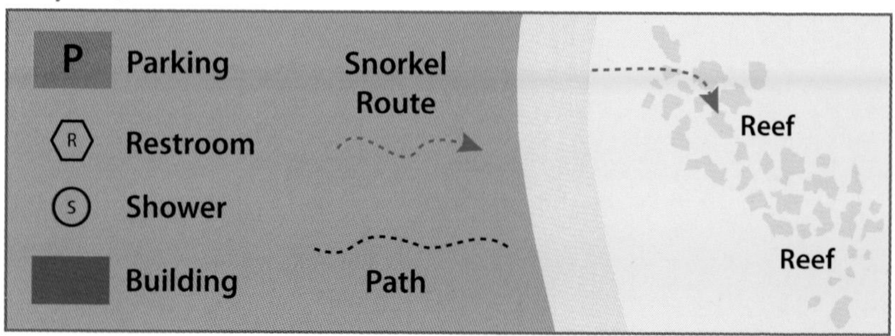

Green Sea Turtle

Maui's Best Spots

Maui is blessed with a ton of great snorkel spots and choosing where to venture can be a difficult task. In the following guides, you'll find candid assessments, advice, and directions to Maui's best spots. If you have a place in mind, read about it first and you'll have all the information you need for a fun and hassle-free adventure. Each location includes a detailed map so you'll know how to get there, where to park, which direction to snorkel, and where to find the closest restrooms and showers. For visitors new to Maui, you'll find additional road maps to help you navigate your way around the island.

If you're not sure where to start, the following lists will get you headed in the right direction. The selections are based on where I would personally take someone depending on swimming ability, snorkeling skills, endurance, and a few other site specific considerations. Not every spot is right for every person. Five Caves - Five Graves is fantastic, but it's definitely not for beginners or young kids. Black Rock is interesting, but can be incredibly crowded. So use the following lists to generate ideas, then read the location guide to get to know the spot. Before your first trip, take a few moments to read the Hazards and Snorkeling Tips sections to stay safe and get the most out of your snorkeling experience.

Maui's Top Spots

Honolua Bay
Five Caves - Five Graves
Maluaka Beach
Ahihi Bay
Olowalu – MM14

West Maui's Best

Honolua Bay
Olowalu – MM14
Coral Gardens
Kahekili Beach Park
Kapalua Bay

South Maui's Best

Five Caves - Five Graves
Maluaka Beach
Ahihi Bay
Wailea Beach
Palauea Beach - White Rock

Best for Beginners
Ulua Beach
Kapalua Bay
Kama'ole I
Kahekili Beach Park
Maluaka

Best for Advanced
Five Caves - Five Graves
Coral Gardens
Maluaka to Black Sand Beach
Palauea Beach - White Rock
Honolua Bay

Best for Kids
Ulua Beach
Kapalua Bay
Kama'ole I
Kahekili Beach Park
Maluaka

Best "Marathon Adventures"
Makena Landing to Chang's Beach
Mokule'ia Bay to Honolua Bay
Little Beach to Black Sand Beach
Maluaka to Black Sand Beach
Ahihi Bay to Ahihi Reserve Boundary
Coral Gardens

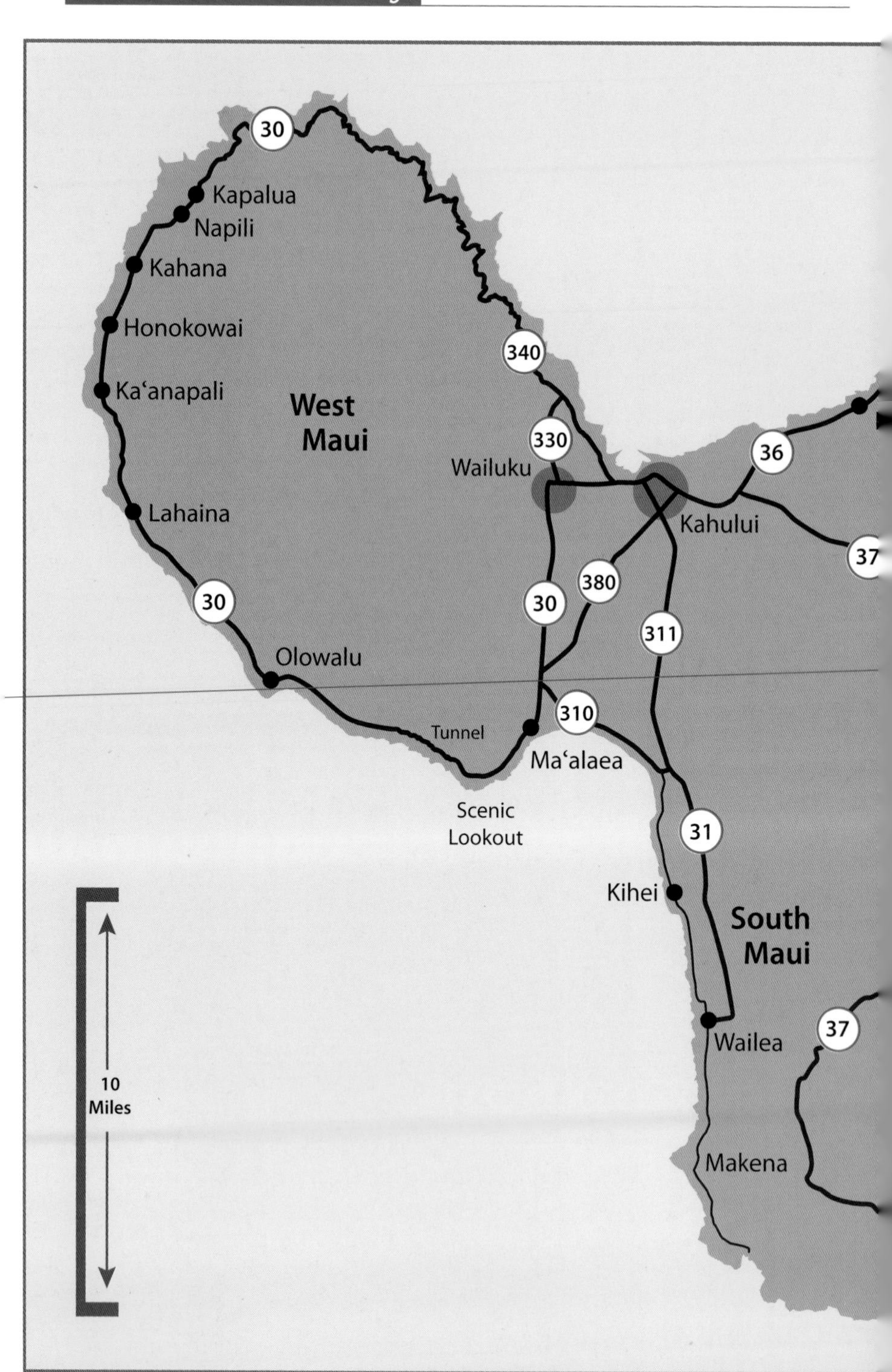
30
Kapalua
Napili
Kahana
Honokowai
Ka'anapali
West Maui
340
330
Wailuku
36
Kahului
Lahaina
37
380
30
30
311
Olowalu
310
Tunnel
Ma'alaea
Scenic Lookout
31
Kihei
South Maui
10 Miles
Wailea
37
Makena

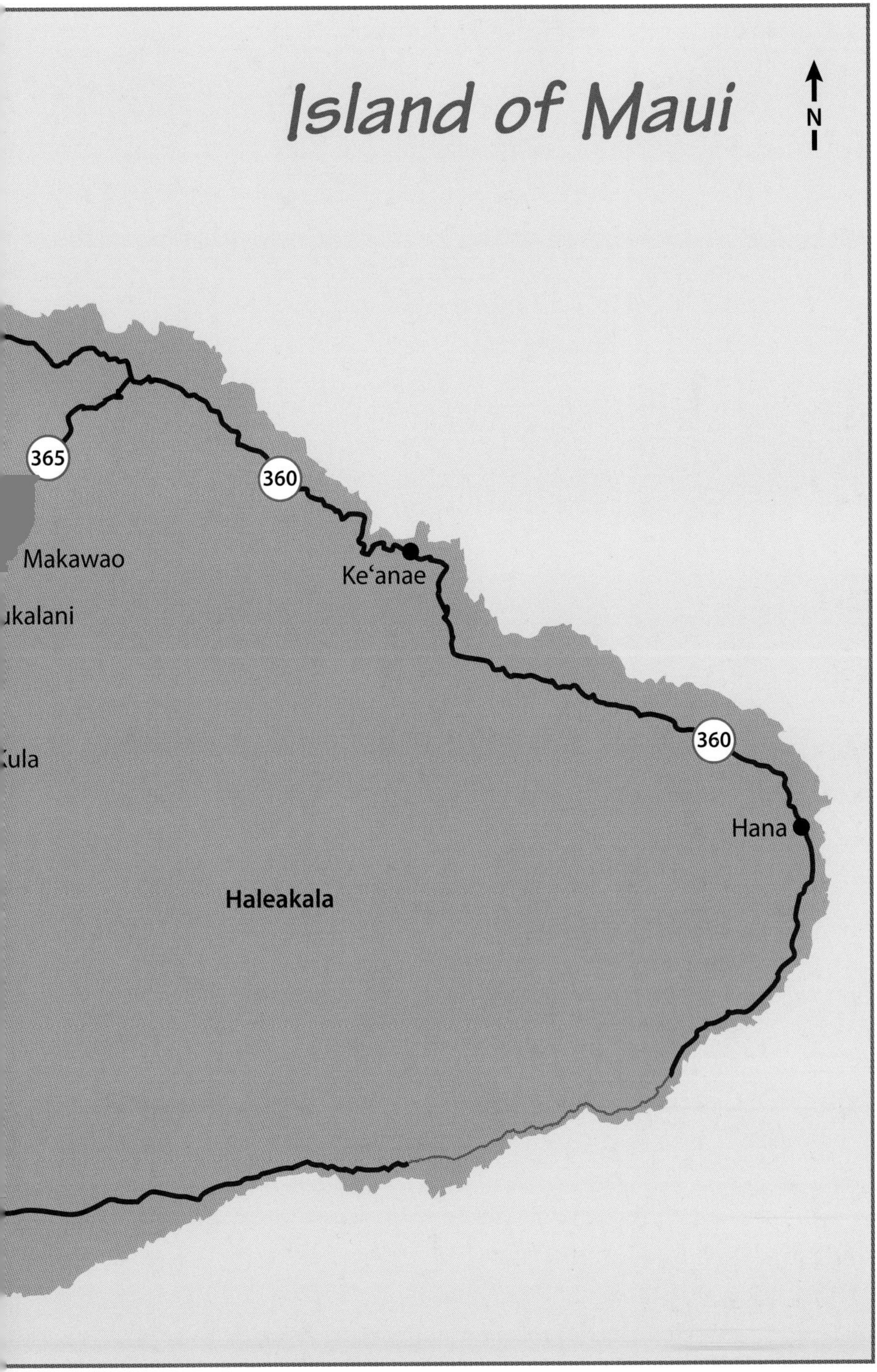

Island of Maui

N
365
360
Makawao
Keʻanae
ukalani
ula
360
Hana
Haleakala

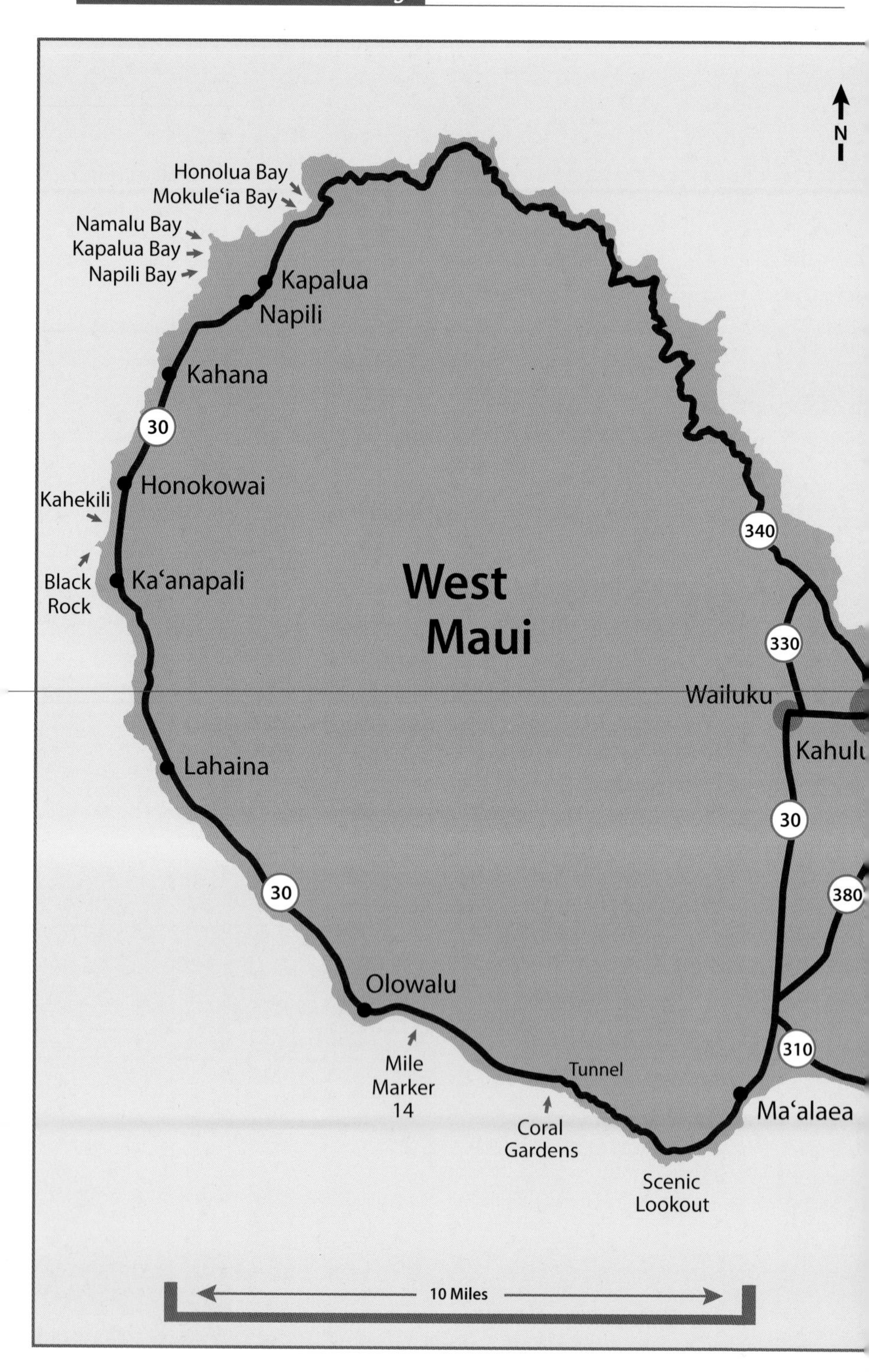

N
Honolua Bay
Mokule'ia Bay
Namalu Bay
Kapalua Bay
Napili Bay
Kapalua
Napili
Kahana
30
Honokowai
Kahekili
Black Rock
Ka'anapali
West Maui
340
330
Wailuku
Kahulu
Lahaina
30
30
380
Olowalu
Mile Marker 14
Tunnel
Coral Gardens
310
Ma'alaea
Scenic Lookout
10 Miles

Canoe Beach

West Maui Road Maps

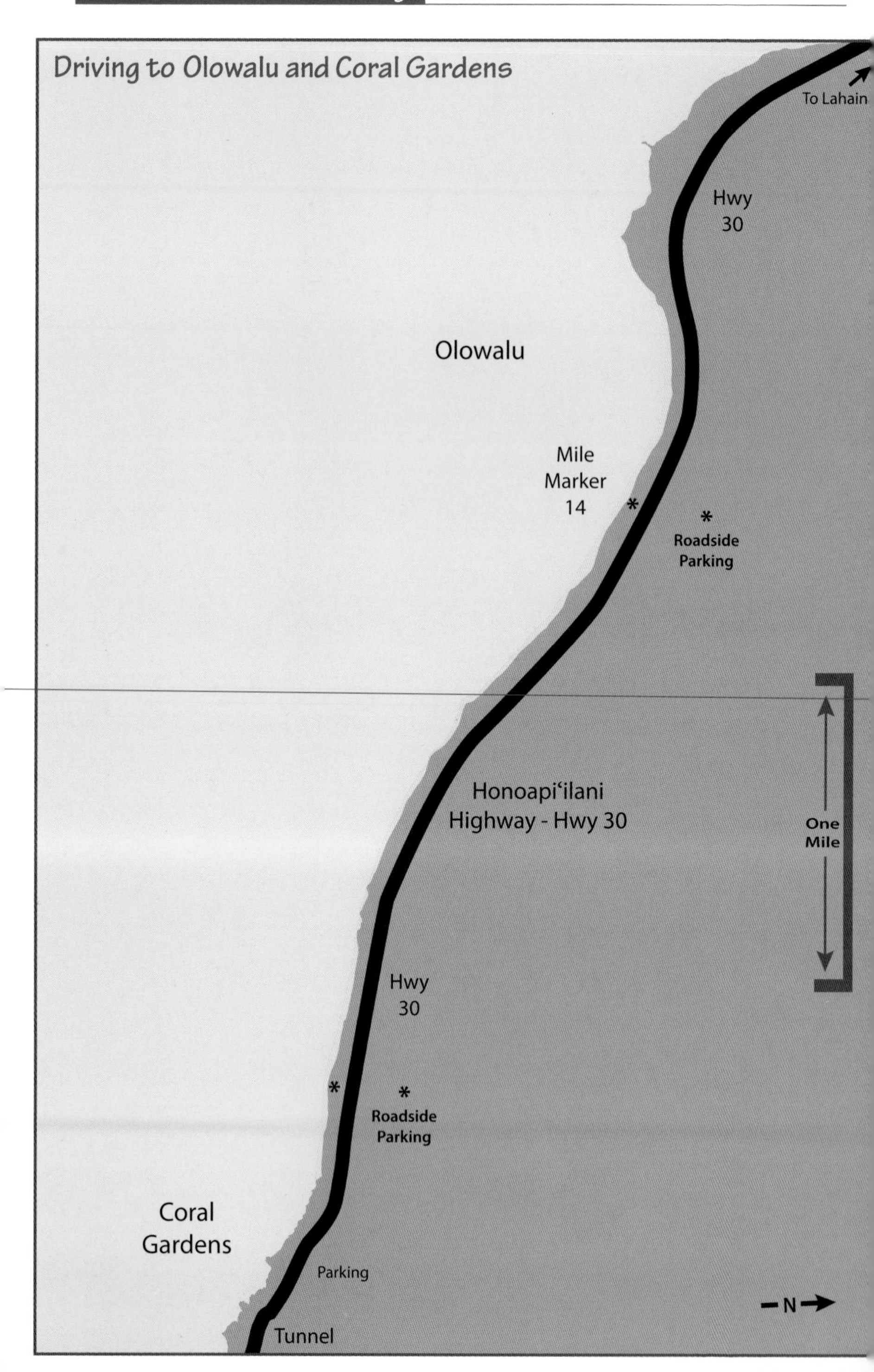

Driving to Olowalu and Coral Gardens
To Lahain
Hwy
30
Olowalu
Mile
Marker
14
Roadside
Parking
Honoapi'ilani
Highway - Hwy 30
One
Mile
Hwy
30
Roadside
Parking
Coral
Gardens
Parking
Tunnel
N

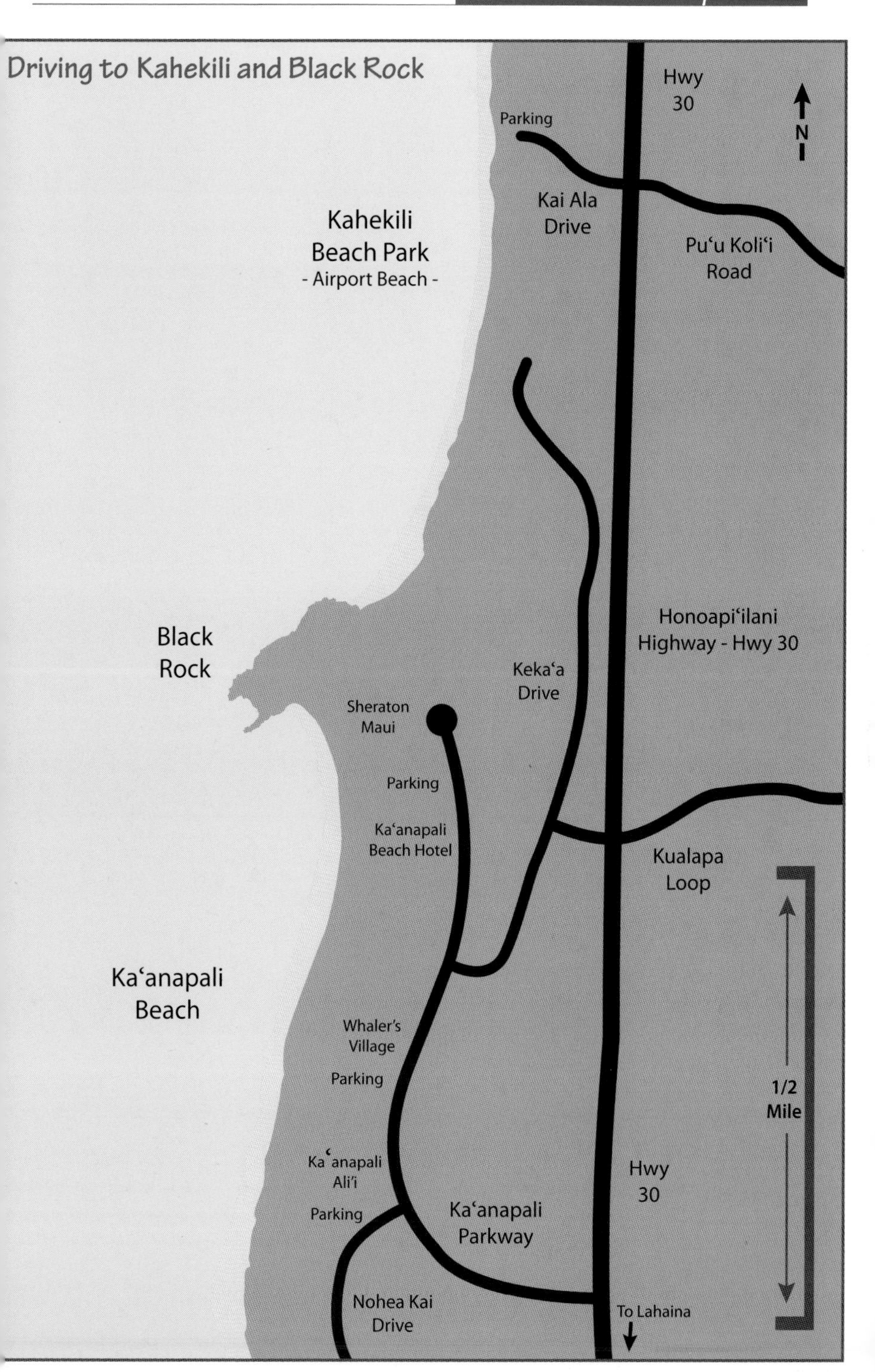
Driving to Kahekili and Black Rock
Hwy 30
N
Parking
Kai Ala Drive
Kahekili Beach Park
- Airport Beach -
Pu'u Koli'i Road
Honoapi'ilani Highway - Hwy 30
Black Rock
Keka'a Drive
Sheraton Maui
Parking
Ka'anapali Beach Hotel
Kualapa Loop
Ka'anapali Beach
Whaler's Village
Parking
1/2 Mile
Ka'anapali Ali'i
Parking
Hwy 30
Ka'anapali Parkway
Nohea Kai Drive
To Lahaina

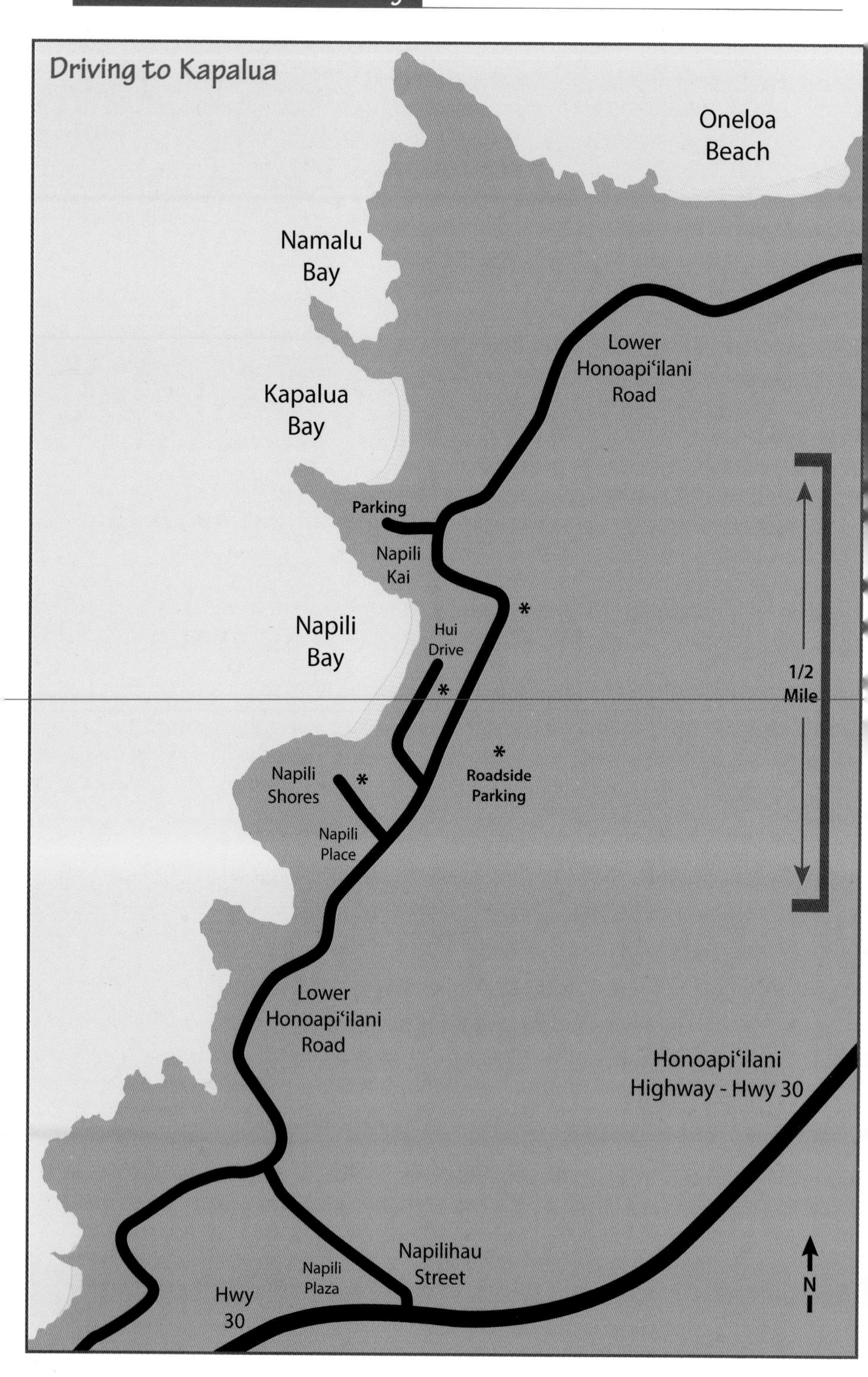

Driving to Kapalua
Oneloa Beach
Namalu Bay
Lower Honoapi'ilani Road
Kapalua Bay
Parking
Napili Kai
Napili Bay
Hui Drive
1/2 Mile
Napili Shores
Roadside Parking
Napili Place
Lower Honoapi'ilani Road
Honoapi'ilani Highway - Hwy 30
Napilihau Street
Napili Plaza
Hwy 30
N

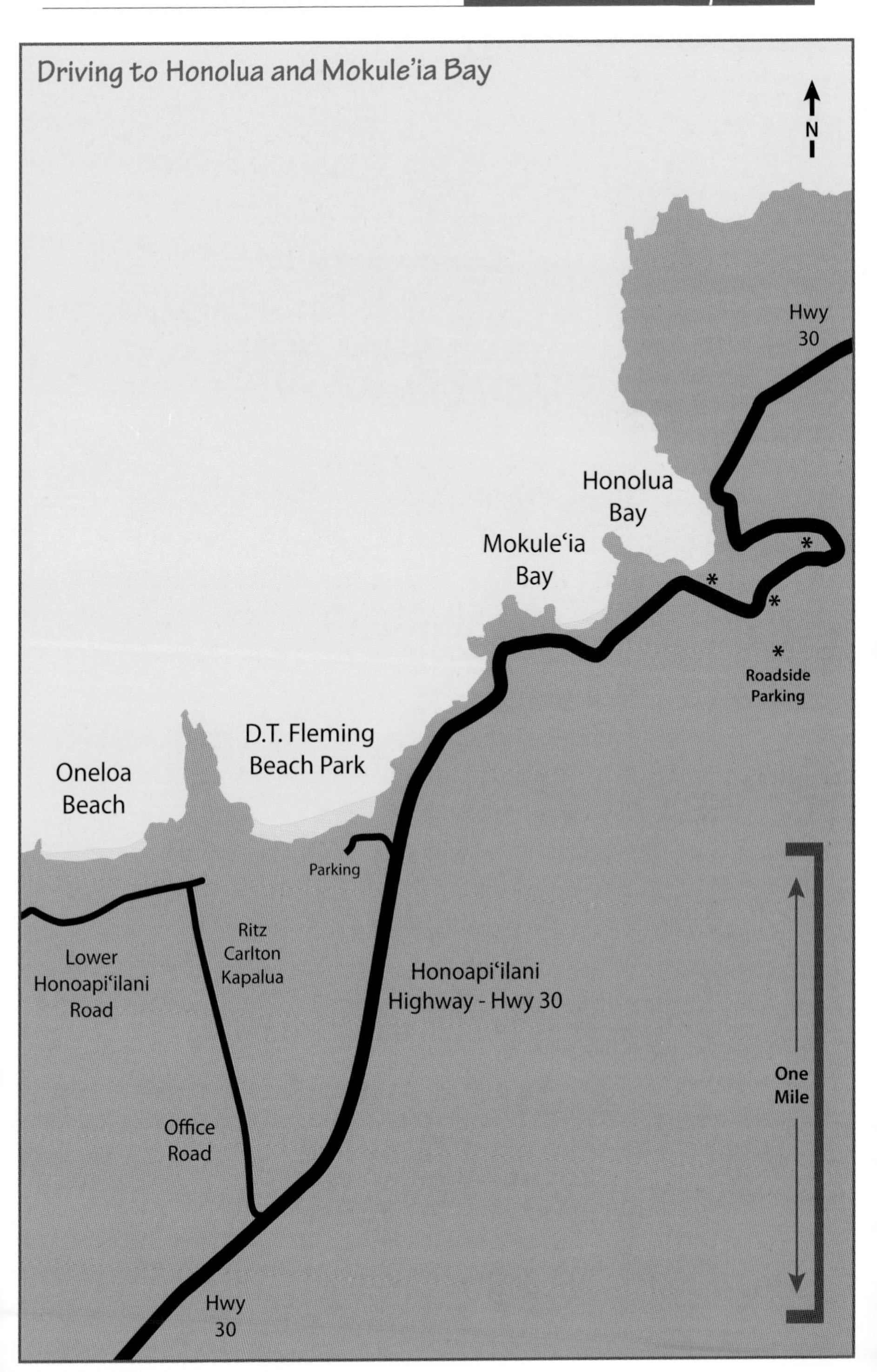

Driving to Honolua and Mokule'ia Bay
N
Hwy 30
Honolua Bay
Mokule'ia Bay
*
*
*
*
Roadside Parking
D.T. Fleming Beach Park
Oneloa Beach
Parking
Ritz Carlton Kapalua
Lower Honoapi'ilani Road
Honoapi'ilani Highway - Hwy 30
Office Road
One Mile
Hwy 30

Honolua Bay

Honolua Bay can offer some of the best snorkeling found on Maui. When the waters are calm and there's no run-off from a recent rain, the clarity can be exceptional. Additionally, since it's a designated marine preserve and fishing isn't allowed, you'll often find great fish counts and see some exceptionally large fish. I once came upon a pufferfish here the size of a small dog.

The bay offers a large horseshoe shape to explore. Both sides are interesting, but the right side is decidedly better with its coral reefs and abundant marine life. The left side has less coral but offers interesting rocky outcroppings and crevices to investigate. A deep sandy channel in the middle of the bay separates the two sides and requires a healthy swim to snorkel both areas during a single outing. There's not much to see as you swim over this "sand desert" and it's easy to get tired or cold so you may want to take a break before exploring the other side.

Embraced by cliffs on two sides, Honolua is backed by a jungle that gives it a remote and tropical feel. While the shore doesn't provide the sandy beaches found most everywhere else on Maui, the jumble of large rocks surrounding the bay provide reasonable resting spots for you and your gear. With the help of a well-placed snorkel fin, your towel, and backpack, you can even get comfortable enough to take a nap. After an

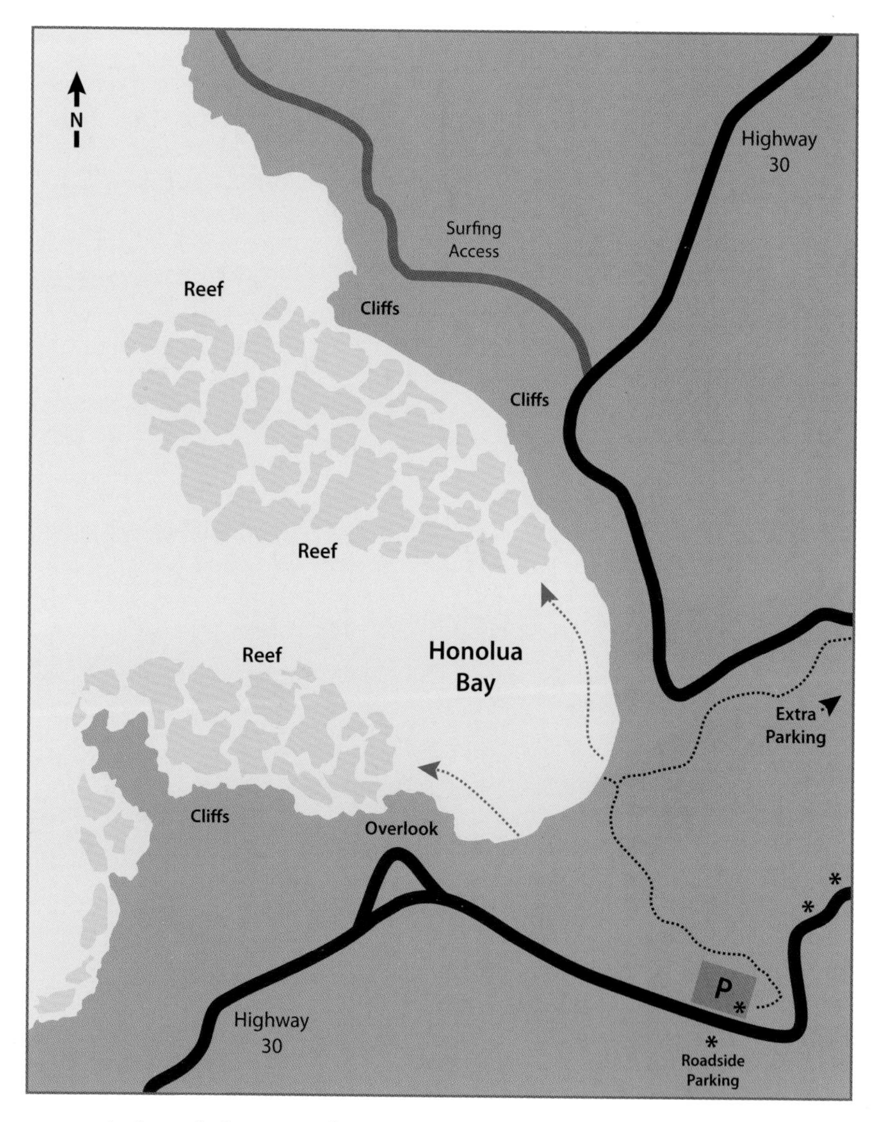

extended snorkel outing, it's a peaceful spot to soak up the sun and chase off the chill while water laps against the rocks. Some might even call it heaven—I know I do.

Facilities: Other than one portable restroom located at the second parking area, there are no restrooms or showers at Honolua Bay. The closest amenities are about a mile back toward Kapalua at DT Fleming Beach Park.

Snorkeling: Most visitors enter the water from the shallow area near the remnants of an old cement boat ramp, but be careful as the cement can be slippery. The water is often cloudy here and the rocky shores of Honolua Bay provide prime habitat for sea urchins so be on alert as you enter and exit the bay. Once in the water, choose a direction and hug the shoreline for about 20 yards. You'll soon be among fish, coral, or both. Water clarity, fish counts, and coral only get better the further you venture.

The initial sandy bottom may appear barren, but be sure to scan your surroundings carefully. Among the scattered rocks I've spotted octopus, flounder, and schools of Bigfin Squid. Squid are beautiful and intriguing to watch. They'll hover leisurely, changing color and shape in unison for 10 minutes, then in a "blink of an eye" they're gone. While watching a group of Bigfin one day, I took shot after shot with my underwater camera. Taking a moment to check a setting, I looked up and realized they'd vanished in those few seconds of distraction. They're amazing creatures and hopefully you'll have the good fortune of seeing them at Honolua. Afterwards you may have second thoughts about eating calamari.

Bigfin Squid at Honolua Bay

If you don't mind hoofing it over the shoreline rocks, skip the initial entry point and take a right. Continue on a hundred yards or so and look for a spot shallow enough for entry, but deep enough to provide clearance over the rocks once you're in the water. It's a little tricky as the rocks can be slippery and urchins are ever-present, but accessing the bay further from the ramp will get you away from the crowds and closer to the best snorkeling. As soon as you're able, put on your mask so you can be on the look out for urchins.

If you've chosen to snorkel the right side of the bay, stay close to the shoreline as you swim. You'll often find huge schools of silver Bigeye Scad hugging the boulders in the shallows. They form an undulating wall of silvery fish that's incredible to watch. You can always tell when someone comes upon them for first time as exclamations of surprise resound from snorkel tubes, followed by enthusiastic shouts to the rest of their group to "get over here quick."

Scad

The further you proceed, you'll find coral at varying depths, segmented with channels and crevices that host a variety of fish. Take your time exploring and you'll likely see an abundance of life. I frequently find needlefish, pufferfish, massive parrotfish, Bluefin Trevallies, large groups of Convict Tangs, and actively hunting moray eels. In the shallow areas give yourself plenty of clearance to keep from brushing against, touching, or kicking the coral with your fins. Each touch can damage or kill coral and unfortunately you'll see massive coral heads at Honolua that are suffering the effects of careless snorkelers. Please don't be one of them.

The reef extends hundreds of yards out to sea and when relatively calm, the area provides intriguing sea life and hours of endless exploration. If you come upon spots where the water appears blurry it's not your eyes. It's freshwater rising from spring vents in the sea floor and moving through the denser salt water. It makes for strange visual effects and slightly colder snorkeling water.

Follow the edge of the channel along the center of the bay and you may discover an occasional turtle. I've often found them resting here. A hearty swim across the channel will allow you to explore the other side of Honolua. The left side of the bay is more rocky with less coral but is still interesting to explore. If you're feeling particularly adventurous, you can even round the point and check out Slaughterhouse Bay. But if there's much of a current, skip it. The current can make it difficult to get back. Of course you can get out at Slaughterhouse and walk back to Honolua, but without shoes, the trip will feel longer than it is—there's about a half-mile of road and a walk through the jungle before you'll reach your gear on the shoreline.

Exiting Honolua is easier than entry as you can swim up to the shoreline, find a rock to sit on, remove your fins, and ease yourself out of the water. Again, watch for slippery rocks and urchins. Keep your mask on until you're sure there are no urchins lurking about. Once you're done snorkeling and ready to make your way back over the rocks, watch your footing. Extended time in the water can make you feel like you're still floating on the waves and it's easy to take a tumble. We learned the hard way when my wife fell and dislocated a finger. Thankfully an ER doc visiting from Honolulu witnessed the accident and offered his services, popping her finger back into place at no charge. Talk about good fortune in the midst of bad, we couldn't have asked for a better person to help—he even shared snorkeling tips for our next visit to Oahu.

Long-Spined Urchin

Location: West Maui, Highway 30, between mile markers 32 & 33.

From Lahaina, follow Hwy 30 north for roughly 10 miles. When you crest the hill at the Kapalua turn-off, you're within a couple of miles. At the base of the hill you'll see a turn-off on the ocean side to DT Fleming Beach Park. This is a good spot to visit after Honolua. It has bathrooms and showers and offers a welcome freshwater rinse. Beyond the DT Fleming turn-off, you'll enter some sharp curves. Take it slow and start looking for mile markers. Just past mile marker 32 you'll find the parking area for Mokule'ia Beach. A half-mile further, you'll see an overlook for Honolua on the ocean side of the highway. Stop here to check the conditions. You'll get a bird's eye view of the reefs and can plan the areas you want to explore. If the surf is high and the waves are pounding, skip snorkeling and grab your camera. Honolua is a great place to watch surfers and take a few shots. If the waves are minor and the activity appears limited to a few surfers off the point, the snorkeling can still be very good within the confines of the bay. Just keep a healthy distance between yourself and breaking waves and surfers.

Back on the highway and less than a tenth of a mile further, you'll see the first of a couple of parking spots for Honolua. If all the spots are taken, continue around the corner and you'll find more parking and a portable restroom. If these spots are filled, you'll find one more parking area just before mile marker 33.

From any of the parking areas, follow the well-worn trails through the jungle to the shoreline. The paths offer a great walk beneath a canopy of tropical vegetation. Take time to look up and around, it's a place you'll enjoy remembering. Along the way you may encounter a shallow stream to cross. If there's much water flowing, snorkeling visibility may be very poor. Don't hesitate to ask someone before you get in.

Jungle at Honolua

Mokule'ia Bay

Situated just south of Honolua, Mokule'ia Bay or "Slaughterhouse" is often overlooked. Its sandy shores provide a bit of a respite from the busier resort beaches and offer a great view of the island of Moloka'i. While snorkeling isn't as spectacular as its neighbor, it's a nice add-on when you're visiting Honolua Bay. If you're a serious snorkeler and staying in West Maui, it's a must. It features some interesting rock formations, large fish, and is the gateway to a longer snorkel excursion around the point to Honolua. Since conditions can often be rough, this spot is probably best left to experienced snorkelers or swimmers. Entry and exit can make this area tricky. Sizeable waves can crash on shore and there are several large rocks in the surf you'll need to maneuver around. When it's calm, it's no problem. But if the surf picks up unexpectedly, it can be a wild exercise to keep from being slammed into them. If you have kids in tow, it's best to stick with Honolua or head to Kapalua.

For what it's worth, Mokule'ia Bay got its unusual nickname from an old slaughterhouse once located on the cliffs above the bay. Though torn down long ago the name has stuck, perhaps the pronunciation is just easier for visitors.

Facilities: Nearest showers and restrooms: DT Fleming Beach Park.

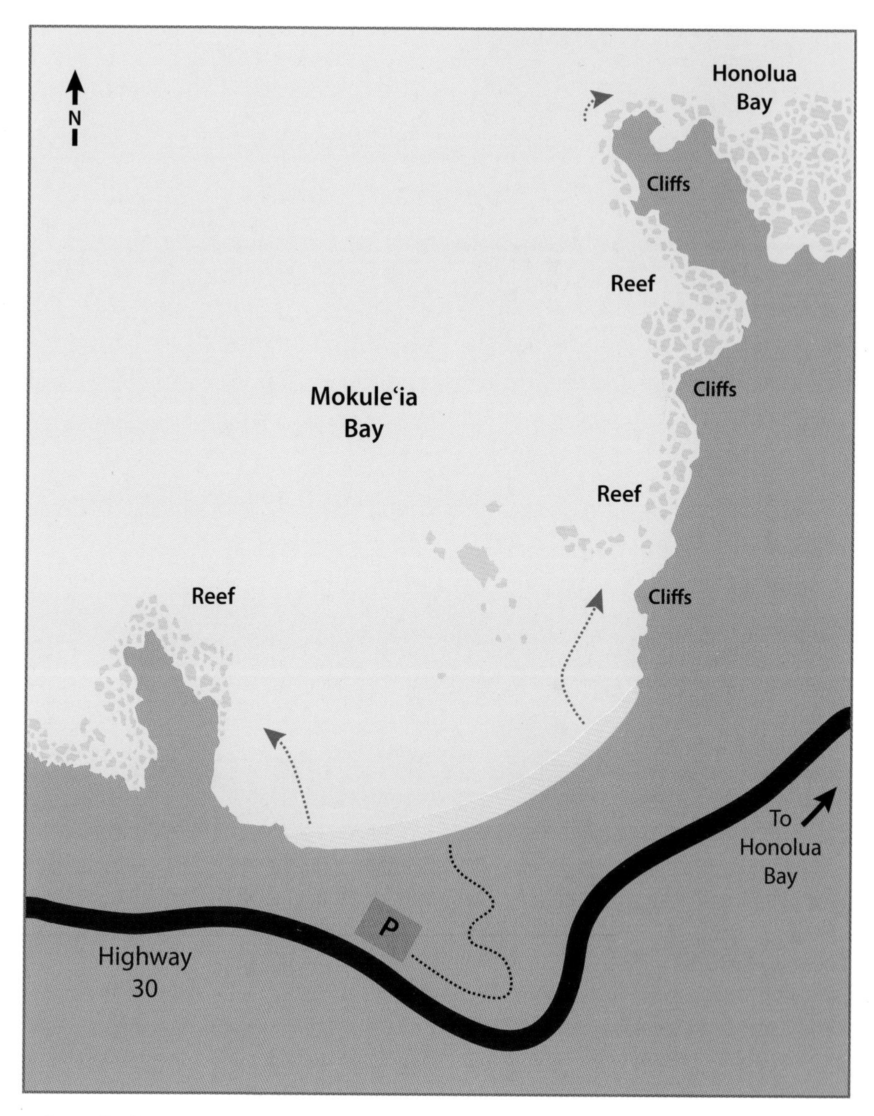

Snorkeling: The beach has rocky points on both ends, but you'll want to snorkel on the right. The left often has poor visibility. When you get down to the beach, make your way to the right and take a few moments to watch the surf and check conditions. Take note of the rocks and plan your entry and exit to avoid them.

Once in the water and well past the breaking surf, follow the shoreline to the right. The area is littered with underwater boulders that create pockets of varying depths. These spots provide great cover for a wide

array of fish. It was here where I came upon one of the largest trumpet fish I've ever seen. Like Honolua Bay, the area benefits from marine preserve status and a fishing ban, confirmed by the size of fish you'll see.

As you snorkel, continue along the right shoreline exploring small coves along the way. If conditions are right and you're up for more adventure, round the point into Honolua Bay. Take note of the current as it can be strong. If it's really running, save it for another day.

Location: West Maui, Highway 30, just north of mile marker 32.

The point between Honolua and Mokule'ia Bay.

From Lahaina, follow Hwy 30 north for roughly 10 miles. After cresting the hill at Kapalua you're within a couple of miles. At the base of the hill you'll see a turn-off on the ocean side to DT Fleming Beach Park. It's a great place to stop and rinse off after snorkeling. Beyond DT Fleming, you'll enter some sharp curves, take it slow and start looking for mile markers. Just past MM 32 you'll see parking for Mokule'ia on the ocean side of the road. Follow the stairs down to the beach.

Namalu Bay

Namalu is a really cool snorkel spot, but it's not for everyone. Windy conditions and surge can make navigating tricky and access isn't the easiest. No sandy beaches here, just rocky bluffs and lava shelves to traverse down to the shoreline. While the coral is not as abundant as other places, the rock formations and sea life make it worth a visit for the experienced snorkeler. I've encountered eels, octopus, and even an Oriental Flying Gurnard—now that's an awesome sight. It looks a bit like a fish sporting bat wings.

Entry and exit can appear challenging and likely keeps most snorkelers from giving it a try unless arriving by boat, which can happen when a snorkel tour pulls in to escape a particularly windy day. More frequently though, the only people you'll see in the water are teens who like to dive from the cliffs on the northeast side of the bay. If you come early, before the heat of the day, it's likely the spot will be all yours.

From Kapalua Bay head north. A long swim around the north point of Kapalua, or a short walk up the paved beach path will get you there. If conditions are calm enough take the swim and snorkel route. Great coral, interesting rock formations, and large fish can be found at the end of the point separating the two bays.

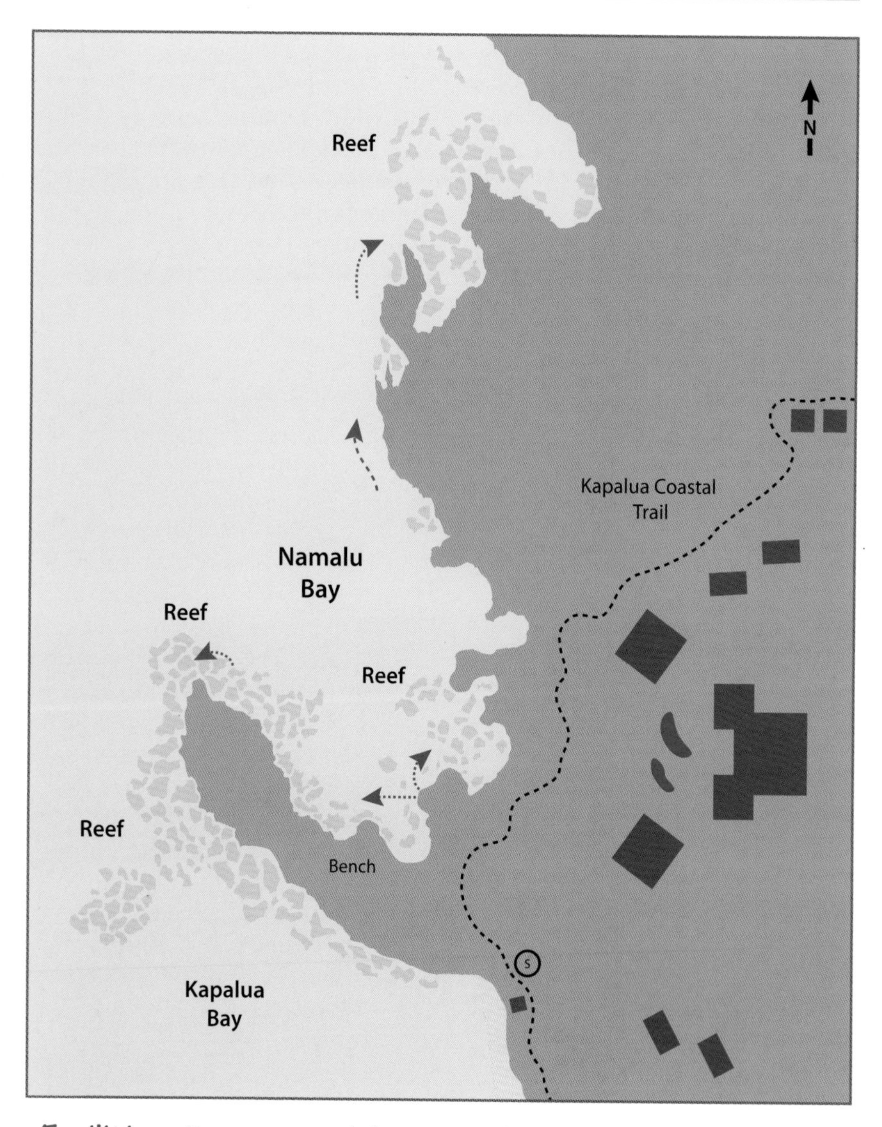

Facilities: Restrooms and showers are located at the Kapalua Beach parking lot. Additional showers can be found at each end of Kapalua Bay.

Snorkeling: Entry from shore can best be accomplished off the rock shelves near the center of the bay. It requires a little agility when climbing over the rocks to get there, but the spot doesn't catch the wind waves more common to the south side of the bay. Once in the water follow the shoreline north or south. Be sure to check out both sides of the bay as they differ considerably and each offers interesting sights.

Proceeding south will bring you to a wider abundance of coral and larger numbers of fish. The initial shallow pools along the shore give way to depths of 10–15 feet with large lava boulders and shelves. Look closely in the crevices of the rock shelves. Whitemouth Morays often reside here. Snorkeling further along the point offers more shelves at varying depths and shallower spots provide ample opportunities for taking pictures of fish. The lighting is often good and the rocks and coral provide an interesting background. When conditions are calm enough, rounding the point into Kapalua is an awesome adventure.

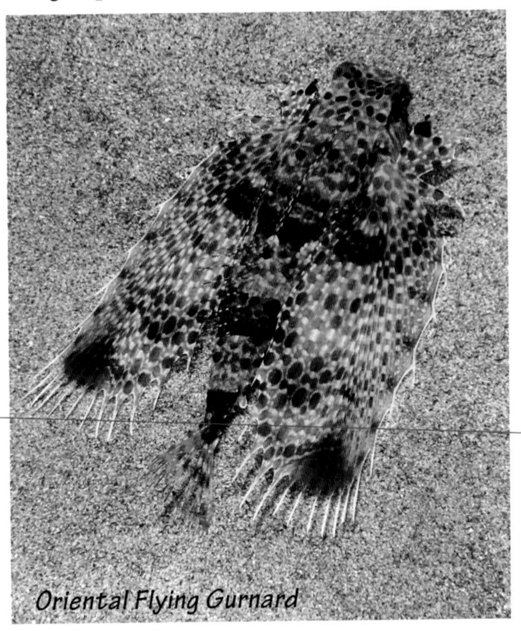

Oriental Flying Gurnard

Snorkeling the northern side of Namalu Bay is much like a wall snorkel. The depths can drop to 30 feet and beyond. I like to follow the cliff wall to explore the nooks and crannies, then float over the sandy bottom and look for interesting finds. Just out from the cliff diving area is where I spotted the Flying Gurnard. In the depths near the northern end of the bay I encountered the largest school of Raccoon Butterflyfish I've ever seen. They were hovering nearly motionless at various levels through the water column—what a sight!

Continuing along the north cliffs, you'll leave the confines of the bay. If conditions are calm, it provides a memorable area to explore. You'll begin to encounter lava rock ledges that break the surface to create pool areas. If the tide is high enough, you can float into these pools and explore. There is plenty of coral as well as a wide variety of fish. Take particular care to not damage anything—clearance can be tight. The further north you proceed, the more pools you'll encounter. They come in various sizes and many are interconnected. If it's too shallow to access them, deeper entries can be found a couple hundred yards further

Raccoon Butterflyfish

along from a small nameless bay. Surge can be rough through here, so again, be careful of your clearance. Very few people explore this area, tread lightly and help keep it in good shape.

Location: West Maui, 8 miles north of Lahaina, off Lower Honoapi'ilani.

From Lahaina, follow Hwy 30 north for about 7 miles. At the Napili Plaza Shopping Center, turn left on Naplilihau Street and continue to Lower Honoapi'ilani Road. Take a right and follow the road for about a mile. After the road makes a sharp left curve, you'll pass the Napili Kai Resort and see beach access signs. Public parking will be on your left. This lot fills early so you may need to park along the road. Follow the walkway past Kapalua Beach. When you come to the grassy point leave the paved trail and cross to the bench at the far edge of the grass. This is a great spot to catch your breath, survey the conditions, and decide your best point of entry.

Kapalua Bay

Rated as one of Maui's most beautiful beaches, Kapalua has it all. The protected bay is bordered with 700 feet of sandy beach, swaying palms, and a meandering pathway through rolling hills of well-tended grass—a perfect place to relax and soak in the view. Even if you don't come here to snorkel, it's a nice place to visit. Grab a late afternoon sandwich at the Honolua Store and bring it here.

For beginners, Kapalua is ideal. Its lava rock arms extend well out to sea and protect the bay from much of the surf. The beach entry is easy, right from the sand, and allows exploration without getting too far from shore. This is a perfect spot for kids. They'll see plenty of fish, some coral, maybe even an eel, and can build comfort and confidence in a beautiful setting.

For advanced snorkelers, it's not bad. While rarely crystal clear, you'll find decent numbers of fish and interesting areas the further out you swim. On a calm day, you can make your way around the south point to Napili or the north point to Namalu. While Napili offers an easy beach exit, Namalu doesn't. So if you're without reef shoes, swimming back may be better than walking. Before rounding either point, take note of the conditions as the current can seriously pick up on either side.

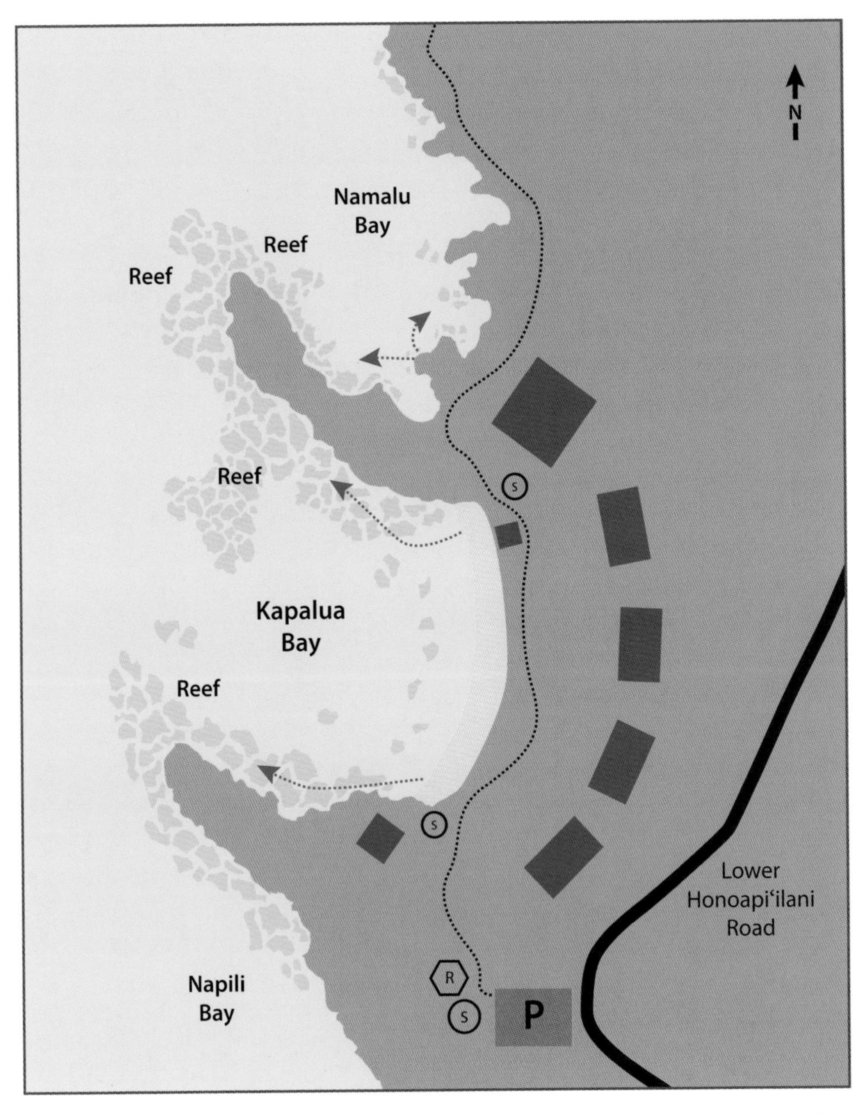

Facilities: Restrooms and showers are located at the Kapalua Beach parking lot. Additional showers can be found at each end of the beach.

Snorkeling: The best snorkeling is found along the north side and far edge of the central bay. Enter from the sandy beach, swim to the right and follow the reef as far as conditions and your judgment allow. Water clarity and reef health tend to improve as you proceed and you'll

encounter some nice coral heads the further out you go. If the waves are kicking up, swing it back around and consider snorkeling the south side of the bay. You can retrace your path or swim straight across. If you choose the direct route, you'll pass over some featureless sandy areas interspersed with pockets of nice coral. It's best to explore widely and see what you can find.

Conditions permitting, experienced snorkelers will want to round the point on the north side into Namalu Bay. It's a great adventure. You'll find a lot of fish and interesting rock formations off the point between the two bays.

Location: West Maui, 8 miles north of Lahaina, off Lower Honoapi'ilani.

Snorkelers at Kapalua Bay

From Lahaina, follow Hwy 30 north for about 7 miles. At the Napili Plaza Shopping Center, turn left on Naplilihau Street and continue to Lower Honoapi'ilani Road. Take a right and follow the road for about a mile. After the road makes a sharp left curve, you'll pass the Napili Kai Resort and see beach access signs. Public parking will be on your left. The lot fills early so you may need to park along the road.

Napili Bay

I love this place. Napili is a pretty little beach that's managed to keep an old-time Hawaii feel. The bay is framed by a crescent of sand and backed by palm trees, tropical plants, and unassuming low-rise condos from another era. It also offers two of the island's best restaurants (the Sea House and the Gazebo), gorgeous views, cooling afternoon breezes, and a great area to play in the water. Unfortunately, and it pains me to say this, the snorkeling isn't too great.

The best place to snorkel at Napili is actually one beach north at Kapalua. I wish it wasn't so, because Napili has a special place in my heart—I learned to snorkel here years ago. But the water clarity is often lacking, the coral is limited, and there's not much to see. If you're staying here, by all means check it out. Explore the points on each side and cruise the reef in the center. You'll find fish, maybe an eel, and a fairly wide area to explore. Just keep your expectations low.

If you're feeling adventurous, you might try the cove around the south point. I've never tried it myself, but I've heard from a Napili Point condo owner that it's actually pretty good snorkeling. If you're considering it, keep in mind there's no beach, it's a lava rock entry, and you'll have to make your way around 300 yards of condo property to access it.

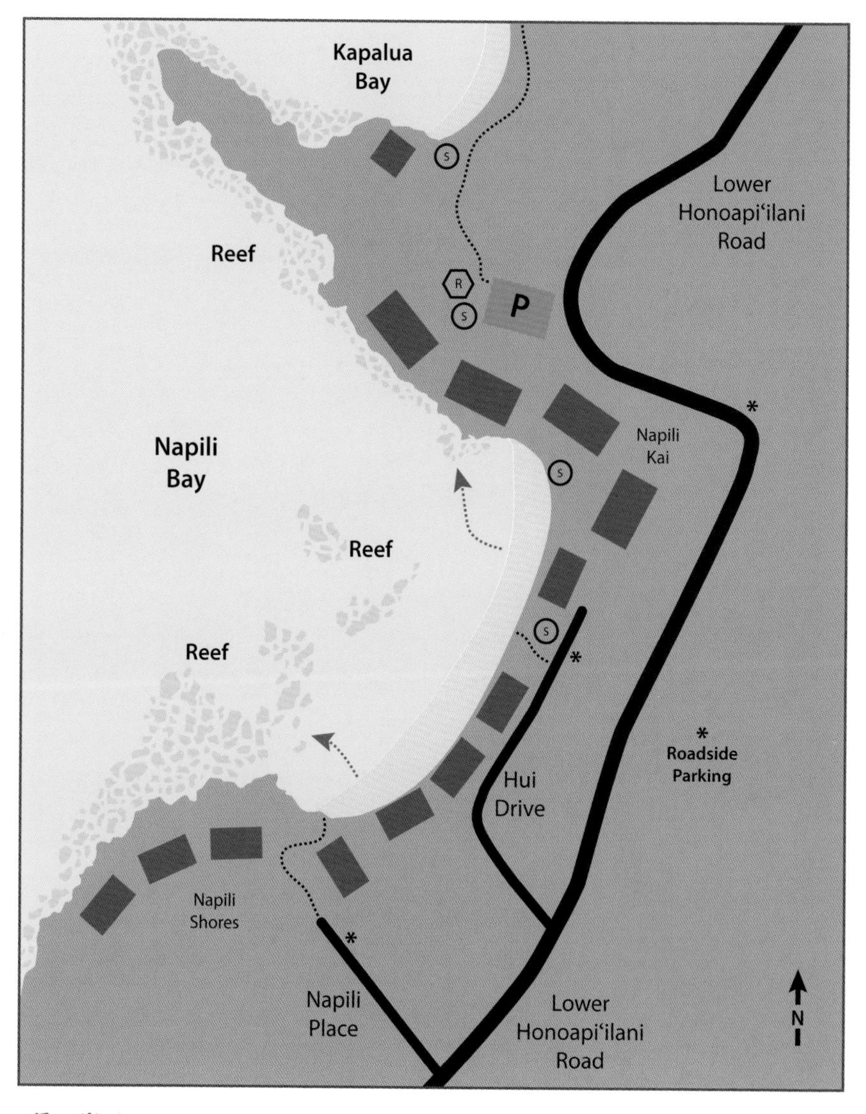

Facilities: No public restrooms. Private showers and restrooms at the various condos and resort. Public facilities are within walking distance at the Kapalua Beach parking area.

Snorkeling: Enter anywhere along the beach and head out to the rocks along the sides or to the reef at the center. It's really a toss-up whether one side is better than the other. If you're staying in Napili and

Napili Bay Sunset

have plenty of time, explore both. Before getting in, this is a good place to really watch the water for a few minutes. The slope of the beach is steeper here than most places and the surf can really pound the shore.

Location: West Maui, 8 miles north of Lahaina, off Lower Honoapi'ilani.

From Lahaina, follow Hwy 30 north for about 7 miles. At the Napili Plaza Shopping Center, turn left on Naplilihau Street and continue

to Lower Honoapi'ilani Road. Take a right and follow the road for a half-mile. Take a left on either Napili Place or Hui Drive. Parking is limited. Look for roadside parking near the beach access points. You can also park further along Honoapi'ilani Road or at the Kapalua Beach parking area.

Kahekili Beach

This West Maui beach park has it all. Its many amenities include a long sandy beach, beautiful shade trees, a giant lawn with BBQ grills, a picnic pavilion, showers, nice restrooms, and plenty of parking—some of it even shaded. To top it all off, Kahekili even has decent snorkeling. It's a well-rounded package that offers the potential for an awesome day at the beach.

Water clarity at Kahekili can be an issue at times, but the ease of access allows you to check conditions quickly and easily. If it's too cloudy for your tastes, take a short rinse under the shower and try another spot. If it's clear you can snorkel the morning away. Additionally, you can also use this beach as a base to snorkel Black Rock from the north side. It requires a half-mile beach hike each way, but when added to a snorkel here it makes for a fun outing.

The reef at Kahekili is close to shore. Starting just below the south end of the park it parallels the beach heading north for quite a distance. Just kick out a few yards from shore and snorkel north. While there aren't huge numbers of fish, you'll find a nice stretch of coral and you're certain to see something interesting. Once while snorkeling Kahekili we heard the faint singing of whales in the distance. It was late in the season but pretty cool once we realized what was making the sound.

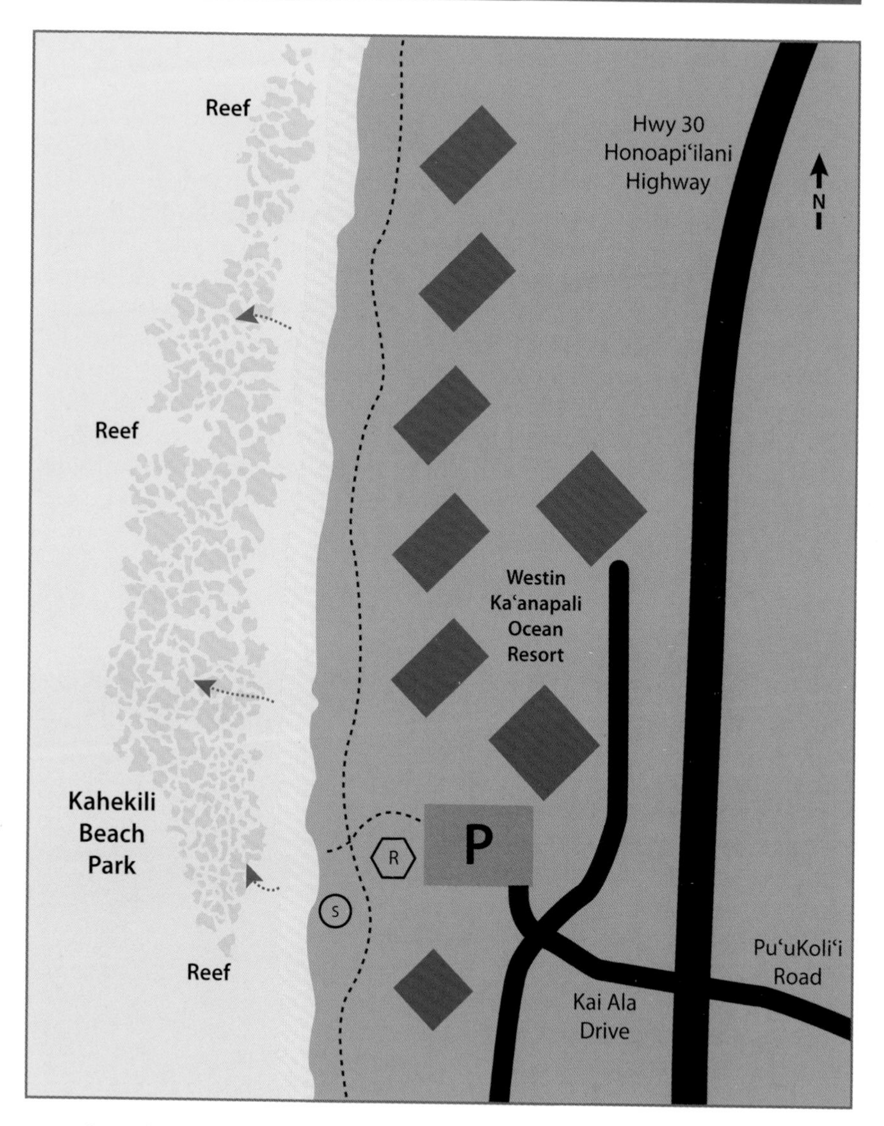

If you have beginning snorkelers in your group, they'll likely feel very comfortable here. It's not too deep and the reef is close to shore. What this beach lacks in adventure it makes up in sun, sand, and fun. Snorkel, stretch out on the beach... enjoy a picnic or a BBQ... then snorkel some more—it just doesn't get much better!

Facilities: Restrooms, showers, picnic pavilion, tables, shade trees, BBQ grills, and more.

Snorkeling: Enter the water anywhere off the park, kick out to the coral and head toward the north. If the current is running with you, just relax and enjoy drifting along. The current is usually gentle and there's plenty to see for several hundred yards. Give a kick now and again to head into areas that capture your attention. When you've had your fill, retrace your path or exit the water and enjoy a stroll up the beach.

If you decide to snorkel Black Rock from here, grab your gear and hike a half-mile to the south end of the beach. Enter the water just before the jetty. Swim along the jetty, round its point, pass the canal, and you'll be at the north end of Black Rock. It's another 400 yards to the beach on the south side. The majority of this snorkel will follow along a coral encrusted lava wall. Mid-way into the excursion the vertical wall gives way to a horseshoe shaped lava shelf. Take care with your clearance and watch for surge. To make your return, retrace your route or take the paved path from the resort grounds back to Kahekili (see map, p. 77).

Location: West Maui, Kai Ala Drive, 4 miles north of Lahaina.

From Lahaina, follow Hwy 30 north for roughly 4 miles. At a quarter-mile past MM 25, turn left at Kai Ala Drive. This intersection is a little funky. On the left it's Kai Ala Drive, on the right it's Pu'u Kali'i Road. Go left, and follow Kai Ala Drive straight into the beach parking area.

Zebra Moray

Black Rock

Black Rock is a popular spot and gets rave reviews from some. I wouldn't rank it that high. The rock formations, coral, and sea life are nice, but the crowds are just too thick for my tastes. It can get pretty bad. I once saw a turtle gather such a swarm people it resembled a celebrity sighting. The poor guy was surrounded. Finally someone displayed enough sense to step back and it escaped. I suspect the turtle and I shared the same thought, "Way, way, WAY, too many people!"

In fairness, the setting here is gorgeous. It's situated at the end of Ka'anapali Beach and backed by the lush foliage and attractive grounds of the Sheraton Maui. It's certainly worth a visit. I just wouldn't go out of your way to snorkel here. If you're staying on Ka'anapali, definitely hit the water with your mask, but get started fairly early in the morning so you can enjoy it before the crowds really pick up.

If you're not staying here, the crowds in the water won't be the biggest problem you'll face. Parking will be—it's limited. The public portion of the Sheraton garage has only a handful of spots and they fill up quickly. The other free lots make for a longer hike. Another option is the pay lot at Whaler's Village. If you buy something in the shops, get your receipt validated for free parking. Just be sure to ask the attendant for the current purchase requirements and time limits.

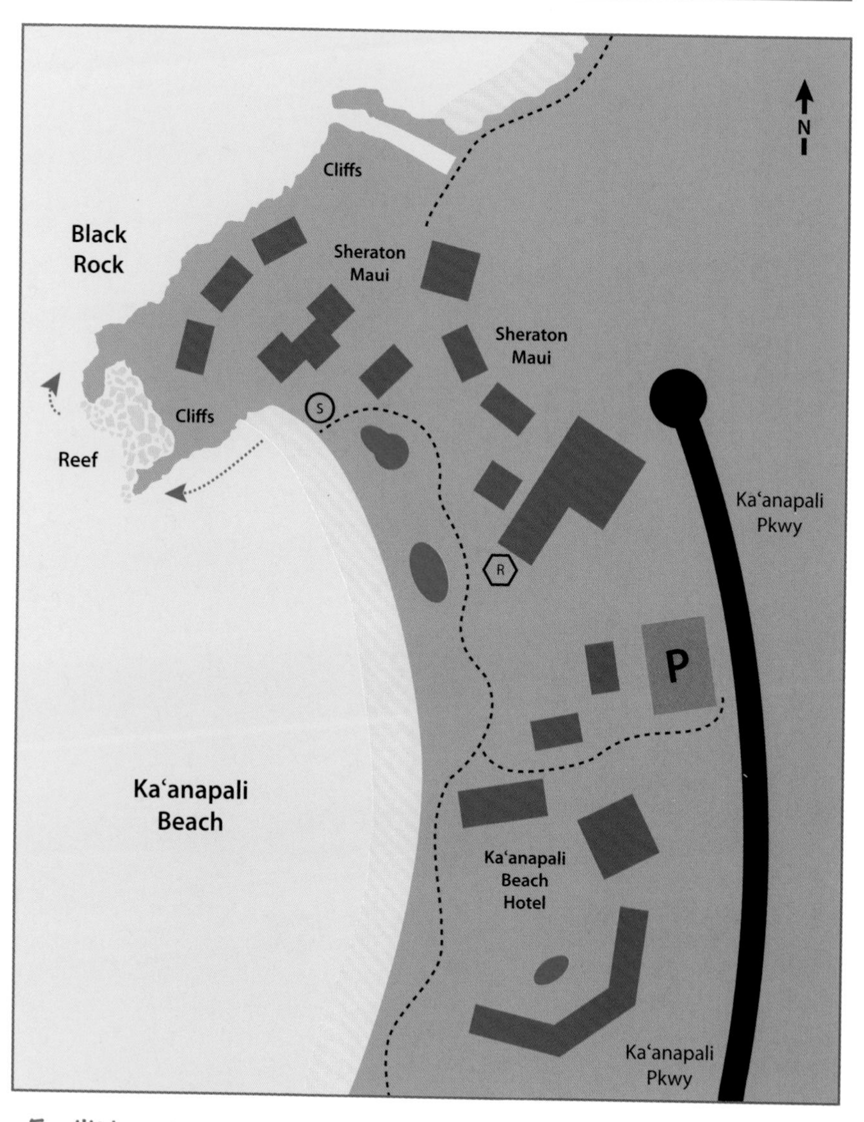

Facilities: Being a tourist haven, there are ample restrooms and showering opportunities along this beach.

Snorkeling: Black Rock is a basic "wall snorkel" along a massive lava outcropping. A hundred yards out, its center opens into a shelf-like bowl as you round the southwestern edge. Depending on the tides and surge, access into this shelf area can be limited and challenging. Another 50 yards along, the wall picks up again and resumes for the remaining

A juvenile Green Sea Turtle prepares to surface.

275 yards of the cliff. As the wall ends you'll reach a canal opening and the edge of a jetty stretching 100 yards out from the beach. The canal is a good spot to turn back. But if you'd rather continue snorkeling around to the shore, a paved path above the beach will take you back to your starting point on the other side of Black Rock. The total distance from beach to beach with a little meandering at the shelf area is just over a third of a mile.

The wall makes Black Rock a unique snorkel that offers a variety of fish. We've also encountered turtles, an octopus, and eels. Once while making our way along the wall a large monk seal passed below us, its speed and grace amazed us.

Location: West Maui, Ka'anapali Parkway, 1½ miles north of Lahaina.

From Lahaina, follow Hwy 30 north for roughly 1½ miles. Turn left on Ka'anapali Parkway. Follow the Parkway to the round-about and swing it around the way you've come. Just past the entrance to the Sheraton you'll see their parking garage. Try parking here first. If the Sheraton's public parking spaces are full continue to Whaler's Village and park in their garage (if you don't mind paying or buying a trinket or two to validate your parking). There are also a few free spots in the parking lot on the south side Whaler's Village and another couple of lots on Nohea Kai Drive just off Ka'anapali Parkway. But if you're forced to park this far away, you may want to re-evaluate your desire to snorkel here. These lots require a long trek up the beach to Black Rock.

Olowalu

Olowalu is a well known spot that seems to always have at least a snorkeler or two plying its waters. It's easy to find, easy to access, and offers fairly calm water with vast carpets of coral to explore. Unfortunately, it has a few drawbacks. First and foremost, coral health and visibility can be awful in the near-shore waters. It clears the further you swim from shore and the coral and underwater relief become stunning. But that brings up another drawback, the "Sharks May Be Present" signs that dot the shoreline. They're a little unnerving and have a tendency to reduce your enjoyment the farther out you swim—cue the theme from Jaws.

To answer the big question: Yes, there have been shark attacks here. It's somewhat politically incorrect to mention, "don't want to scare away the tourists," or "don't want to turn people against sharks." But in reality, there can be sharks here—and a few of them are big, dangerous Tiger Sharks.

Tigers are known to be among the most dangerous sharks on the planet and more than a few divers have reported seeing them in the area. There was a nasty attack a half-mile out by an 18-footer in the fall of 2000, another 100 yards out on New Year's Day 2002, and a fatality back in 1991 about a mile up the shoreline. It's a little unnerving, but

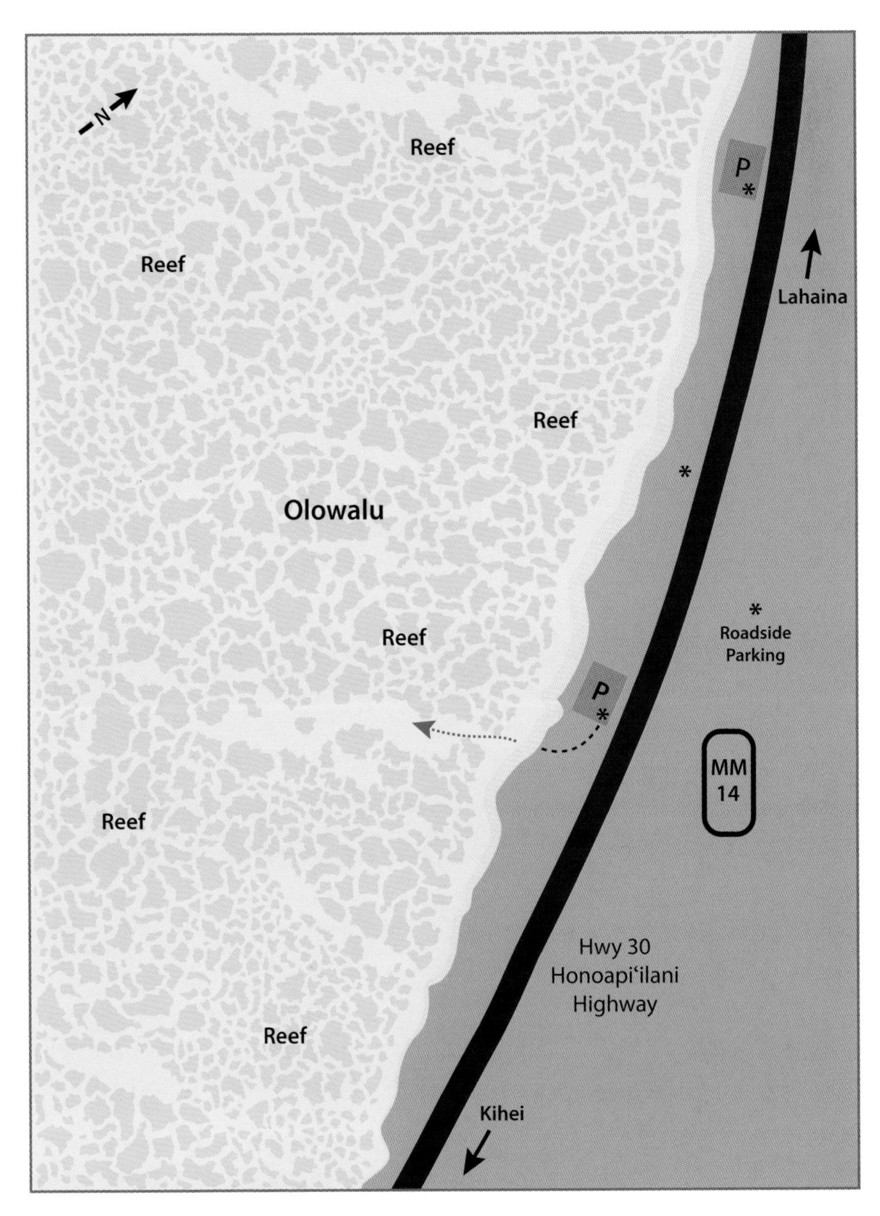

if you put it into perspective, as of this writing that's a 22 year span. If you think of the thousands of people snorkeling here during that time, the numbers are pretty small. And in fairness to Olowalu, there have been sightings and attacks at several other popular Maui beaches. They just missed out on the signs.

Signs posted along this stretch

The best advice for Olowalu is to keep your expectations low and be flexible. If you stop by on a bad day and the water is cloudy, just try another spot. If you're lucky and the water is clear, enjoy the maze of coral channels and beautiful fish. It can be idyllic.

Facilities: Portable restrooms can be found along the roadside.

Snorkeling: The most popular entry point is through the main channel found straight out from the mile marker 14 sign. This entry allows you to get past some of the shallower areas found near shore and access the reef comfortably. Off this channel you can meander above the coral in all directions. It's an extensive territory to explore, but watch your clearance. Some spots get very shallow and become more so with a shifting tide.

There's a lot to see as you swim through the area. You'll find secluded pools among the coral that are connected through twists and turns. These paths are intriguing to follow and play host to large numbers of fish. After venturing along one it may dead end, requiring you to backtrack. Please be careful and avoid touching or kicking the coral with your fins.

As you snorkel from shore, you'll notice that the reef seems endless. It extends for hundreds of yards and the water generally becomes clearer the further you swim. On calm days, it's possible to push to the outer reef where snorkel boats take paying customers. If you decide to go, know your limits, stay within your comfort zone, and remember it's a long way back. The ultimate way to access this beautiful area is by kayak (see Kayak-Snorkel Excursions, p. 172).

Location: West Maui, Highway 30, just south of mile marker14.

From Lahaina, follow Hwy 30 south for roughly 6 Miles. Park on the ocean side of the road near mile marker 14. If you're coming from the south, MM 14 is just over 3½ miles from the north end of the tunnel.

Green Sea Turtle at Olowalu

Coral Gardens

This is a great spot and offers an awesome adventure for the advanced snorkeler. You may have noticed the Coral Gardens below the cliffs just north of the Pali Tunnel. It's an inviting patch of water that often has a snorkel boat anchored in its midst. It's definitely remote and a chore to reach, but as you can see from the road above it's packed with gorgeous coral heads. It also boasts good fish counts. The water is usually sheltered from the winds and is one reason for the prevalence of afternoon snorkel boats. Despite their common presence you can frequently find the area deserted and have it all to yourself. The difficulty is in accessing it from shore, but if you're up for a real adventure, it can be done.

There are three entry points, each with certain issues to consider:

- The first is a nice sand entry from the south end of Papalaua Wayside. It's an easy beach entry, but it requires a very long swim—we're talking a quarter-mile before reaching anything worthwhile.

- The second is from the boulders along the shoreline. It puts you closer to your target area than the beach does, but if waves are breaking on the shore, it's a menacing place to climb into the water.

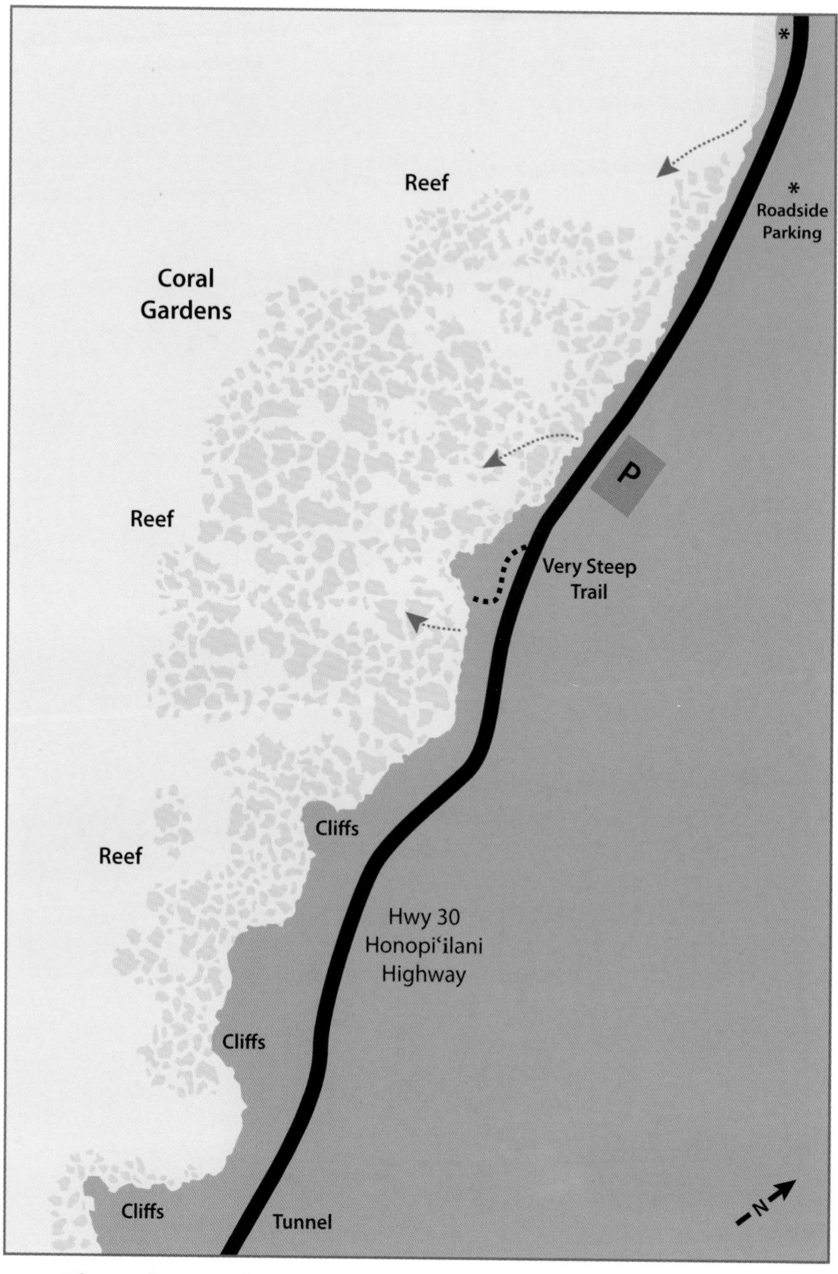

The trail to get there is also less than friendly and hides some nasty thorns. The Kiawe trees offer shade, but they also drop shoe-piercing thorns that have nailed me more than once.

- The third entry is the most direct. It's from the hillside above the cove, but it requires a 200 yard hike along the busy highway and scrambling down a steep slope without a lot of footholds.

My preference is to enter from the boulders and exit from the hillside. If you decide to give Coral Gardens at try, take a look around and follow your comfort level. Whichever route you choose, I recommend bringing reef shoes. It keeps your exit options open and makes for a nice walk back. I carry mine in a mesh bag strapped to my waist.

Blue Spine Unicornfish

Facilities: Portable restrooms at Papalaua Wayside.

Snorkeling: My favored path when snorkeling the Coral Gardens is to swim several yards out from shore and make my way south to the rocky point. Beyond the point is a cove where it's easy to spend a lot of time exploring, followed by a short venture further south along the shoreline. The first cove is definitely the best with a wide expanse of coral stretching well out to sea. The second cove is much less impressive but has an interesting jumble of boulders along the shoreline. Its south side makes a good turnaround spot. Throughout the area, you'll find a wide variety of good-sized fish.

The coral heads in the first cove extend into a vast field 150 to 200 yards out from shore and another 400 yards north. It's a wide-ranging area that tempts the exploring spirit. Enjoy what it has to offer, but pay attention to ocean conditions and your distance from shore. Always stay within the range of your abilities. Remember, you are snorkeling in a remote spot, definitely off the beaten path of a typical visitor to Maui. If challenges arise you are absolutely on your own.

Exiting the water can take some flexibility. If you plan to exit along the boulder shoreline, take note of the conditions before heading back to shore. Observe the waves for several minutes to really get a handle on their pattern. If the waves have picked up and are starting to pound the shore, choose another route. A long swim to the beach trumps a battering on the rocks any day.

If you want to exit from the cove and climb the hillside, the best way out of the water is from the rock shelves off the point. Pick a spot that looks calm enough and work with the waves to pull yourself up and out. Be sure to check for urchins first.

Location: West Maui, Highway 30, just south of mile marker 11.

From Lahaina, follow Hwy 30 south for roughly 9 miles. Parking can be found beach side at the south end of Papalaua Beach Park or across the highway at the Pali Trailhead, just south of the MM 11. The trailhead is a good spot to park if you're entering from the hillside above the cove or at the shoreline boulders. If you're coming from the south, the Pali Trailhead is just under a half-mile north of the tunnel.

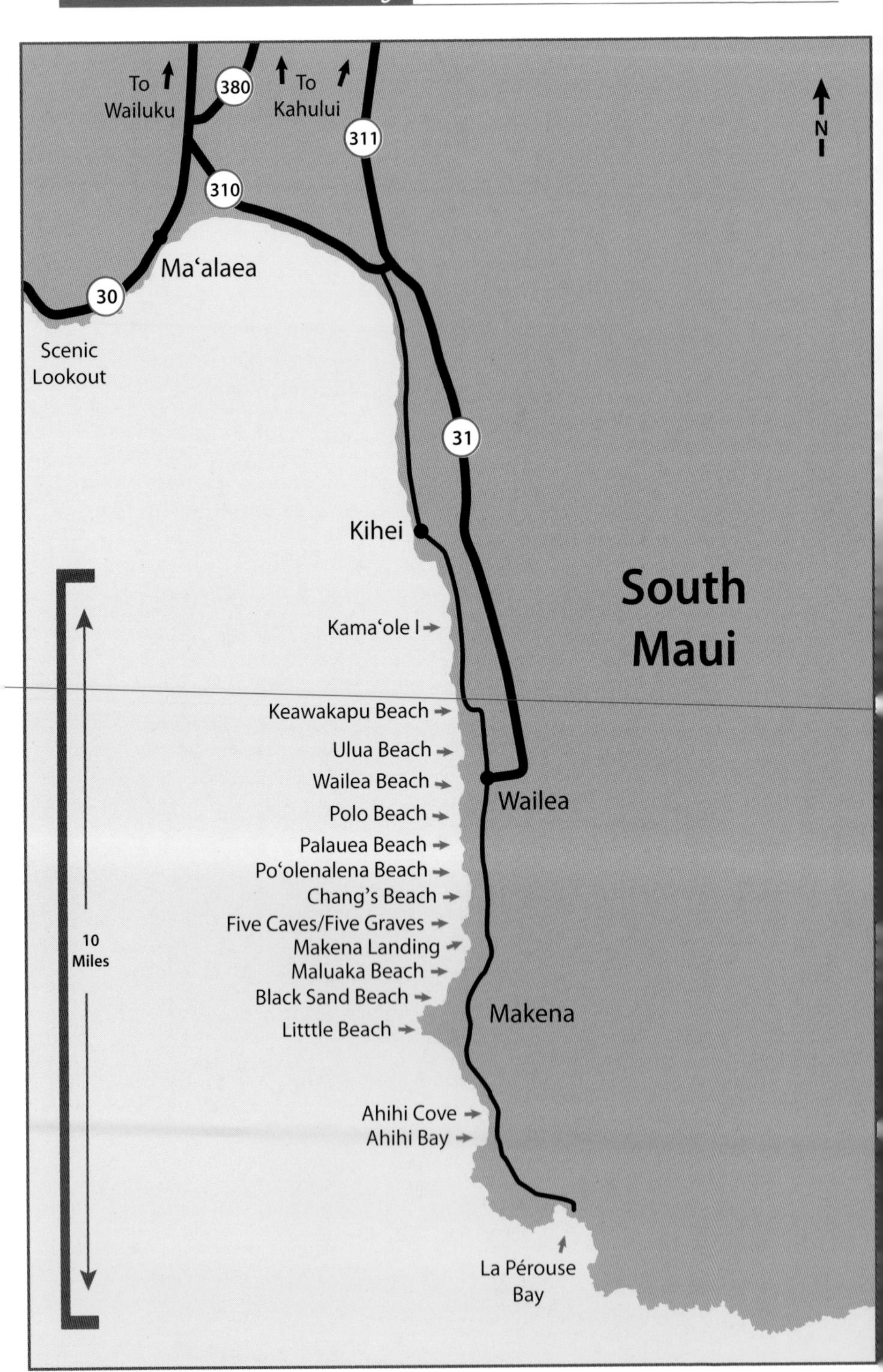
To Wailuku
380
To Kahului
311
N
310
Ma'alaea
30
Scenic Lookout
31
Kihei
South Maui
Kama'ole I
Keawakapu Beach
Ulua Beach
Wailea Beach
Wailea
Polo Beach
Palauea Beach
Po'olenalena Beach
Chang's Beach
Five Caves/Five Graves
10 Miles
Makena Landing
Maluaka Beach
Black Sand Beach
Makena
Litttle Beach
Ahihi Cove
Ahihi Bay
La Pérouse Bay

Secret Beach

South Maui Road Maps

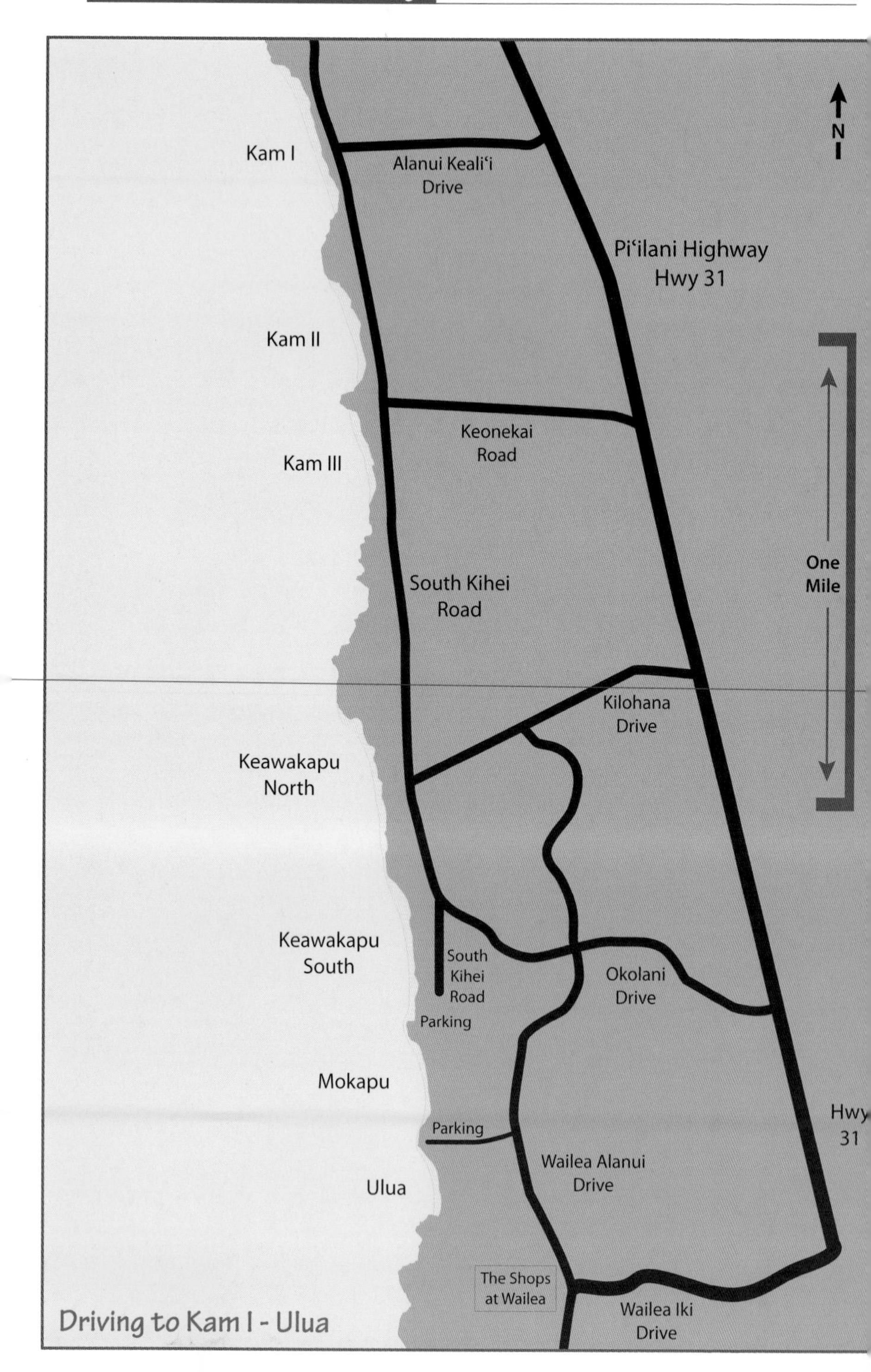
N
Kam I
Alanui Keali'i Drive
Pi'ilani Highway Hwy 31
Kam II
One Mile
Keonekai Road
Kam III
South Kihei Road
Kilohana Drive
Keawakapu North
Keawakapu South
South Kihei Road
Okolani Drive
Parking
Mokapu
Parking
Hwy 31
Wailea Alanui Drive
Ulua
The Shops at Wailea
Wailea Iki Drive
Driving to Kam I - Ulua

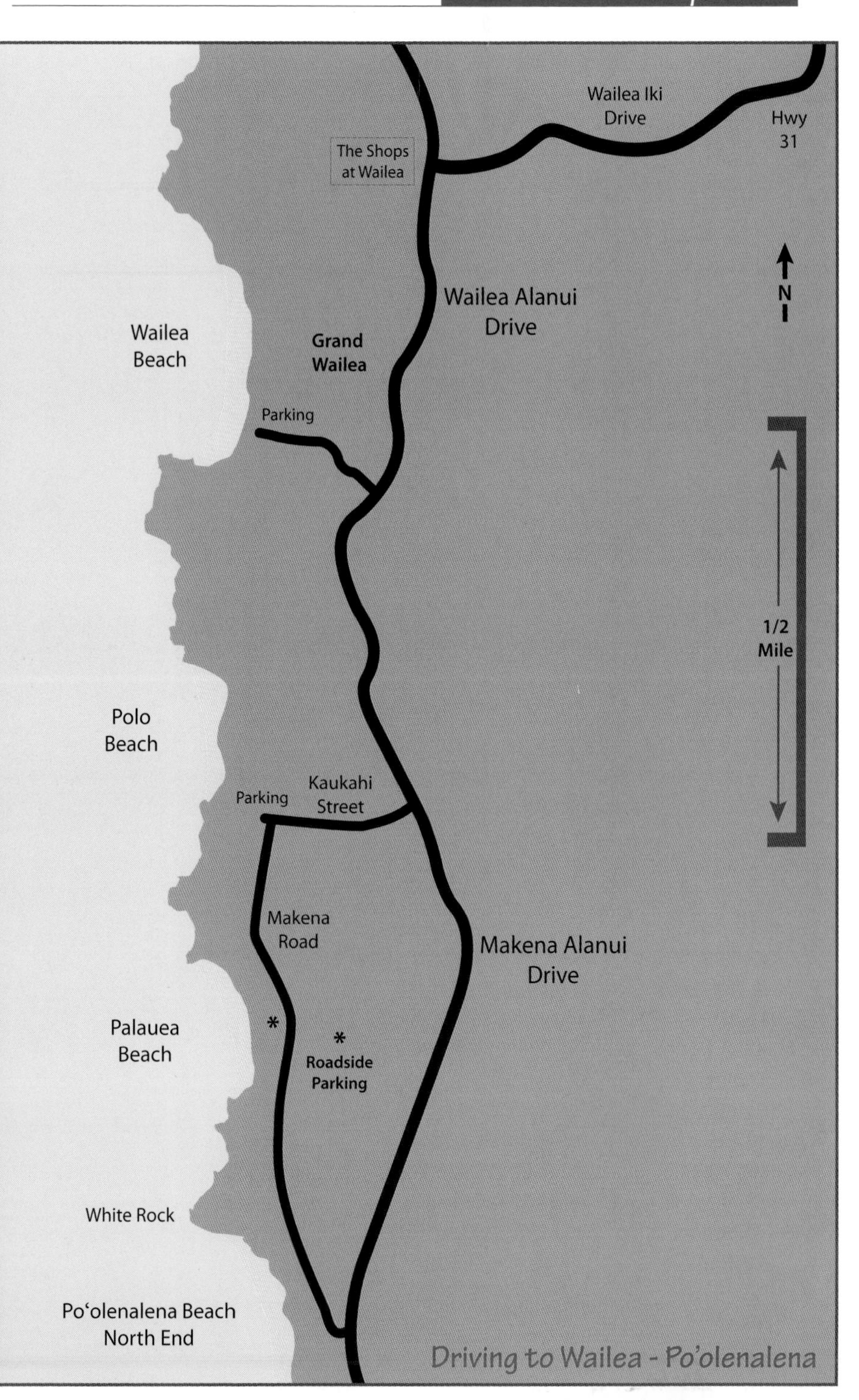

Wailea Iki
Drive
Hwy
31
The Shops
at Wailea
N
Wailea Alanui
Drive
Wailea
Beach
Grand
Wailea
Parking
1/2
Mile
Polo
Beach
Kaukahi
Street
Parking
Makena
Road
Makena Alanui
Drive
Palauea
Beach
*
*
Roadside
Parking
White Rock
Po'olenalena Beach
North End
Driving to Wailea - Po'olenalena

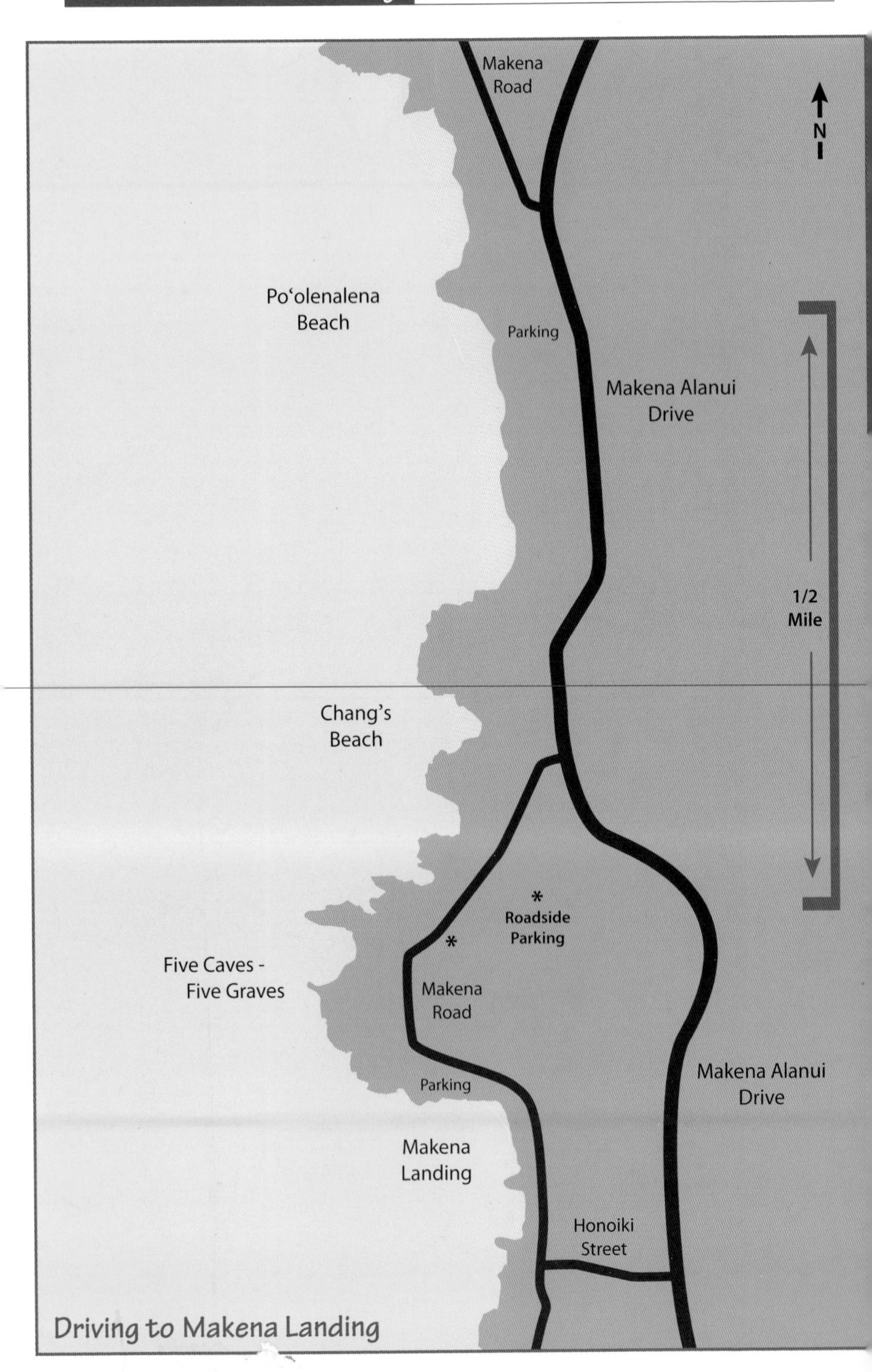

Driving to Makena Landing

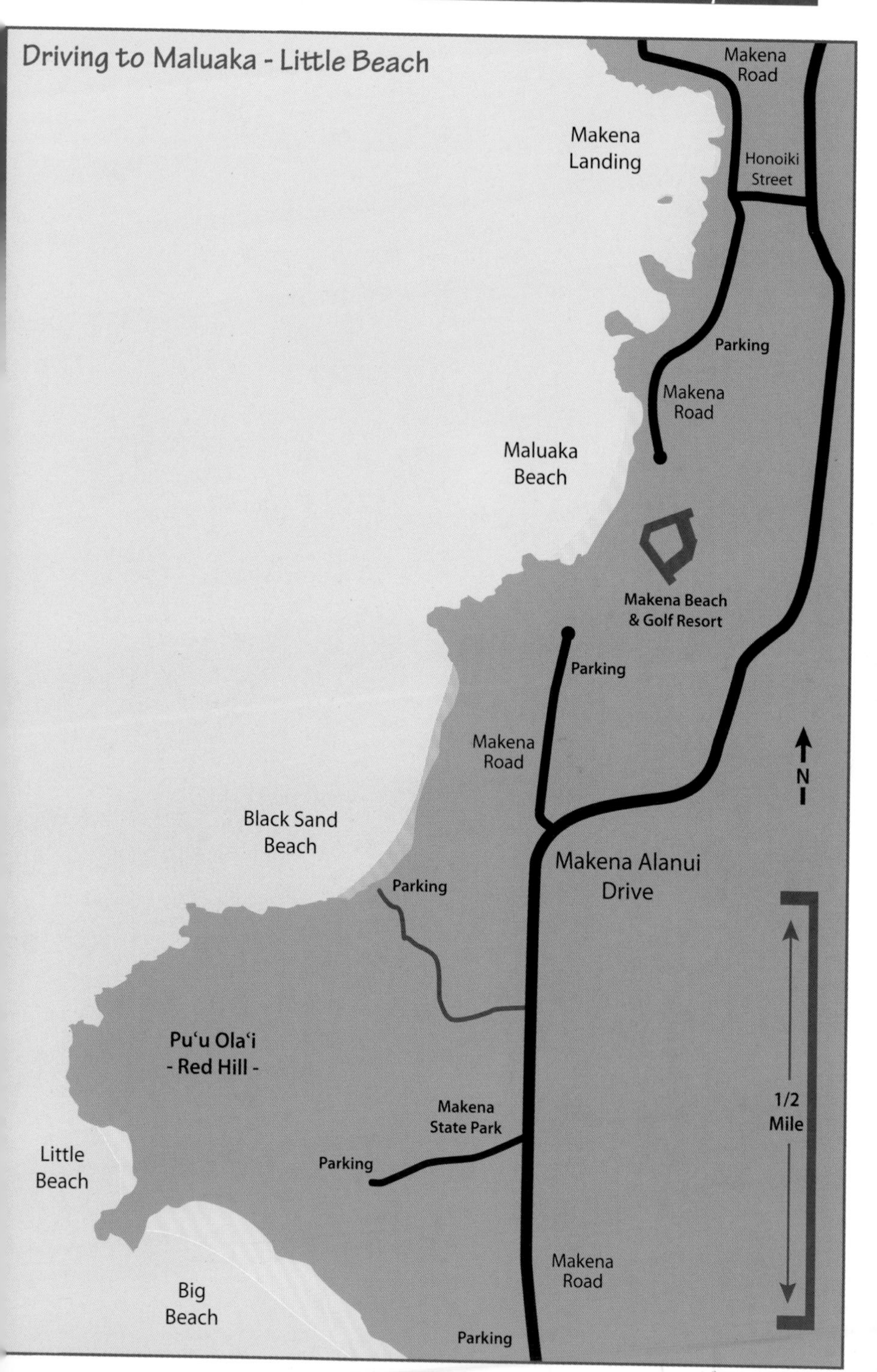
Driving to Maluaka - Little Beach
Makena Road
Makena Landing
Honoiki Street
Parking
Makena Road
Maluaka Beach
Makena Beach & Golf Resort
Parking
Makena Road
N
Black Sand Beach
Makena Alanui Drive
Parking
Pu'u Ola'i - Red Hill -
1/2 Mile
Makena State Park
Little Beach
Parking
Makena Road
Big Beach
Parking

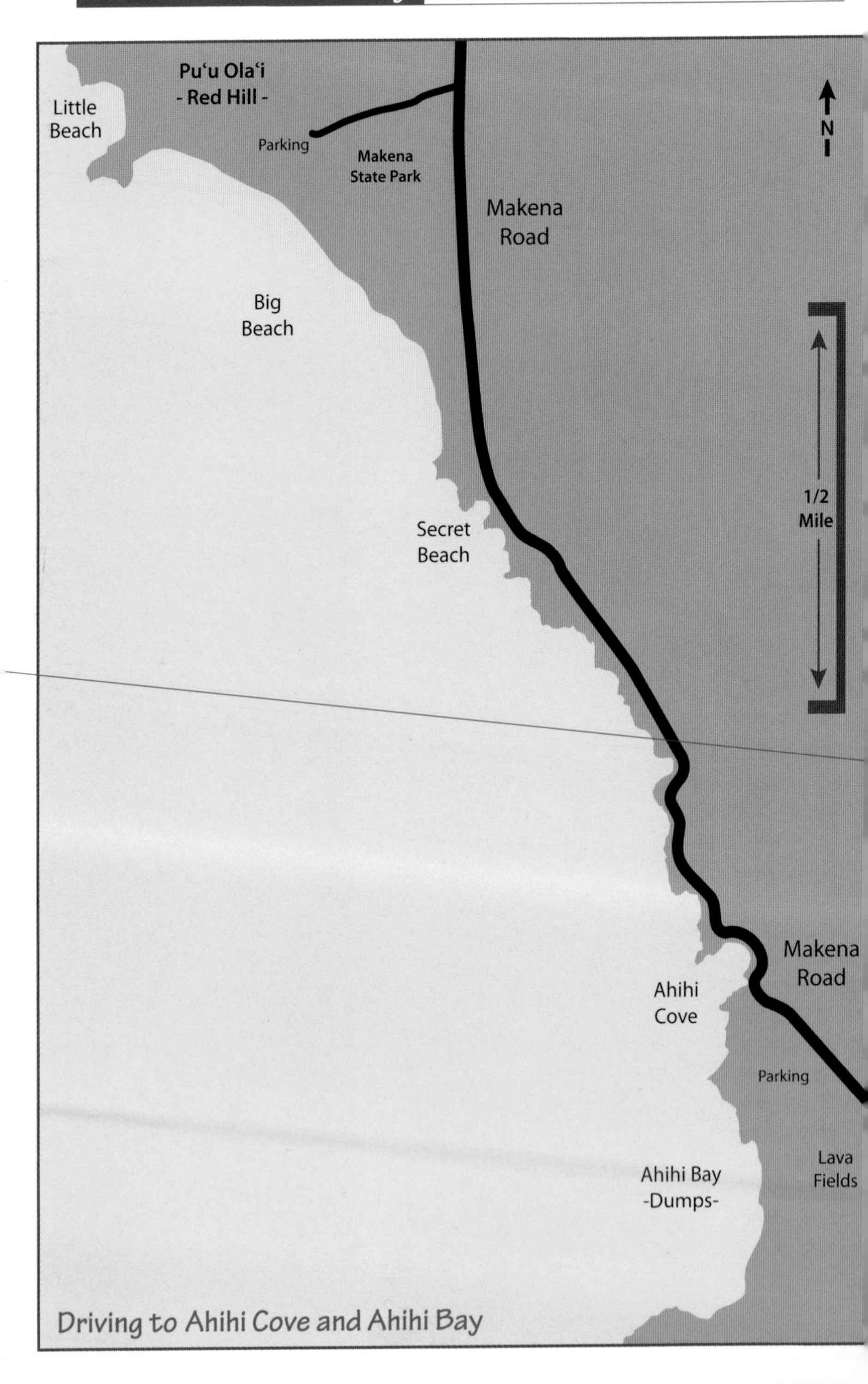

Driving to Ahihi Cove and Ahihi Bay

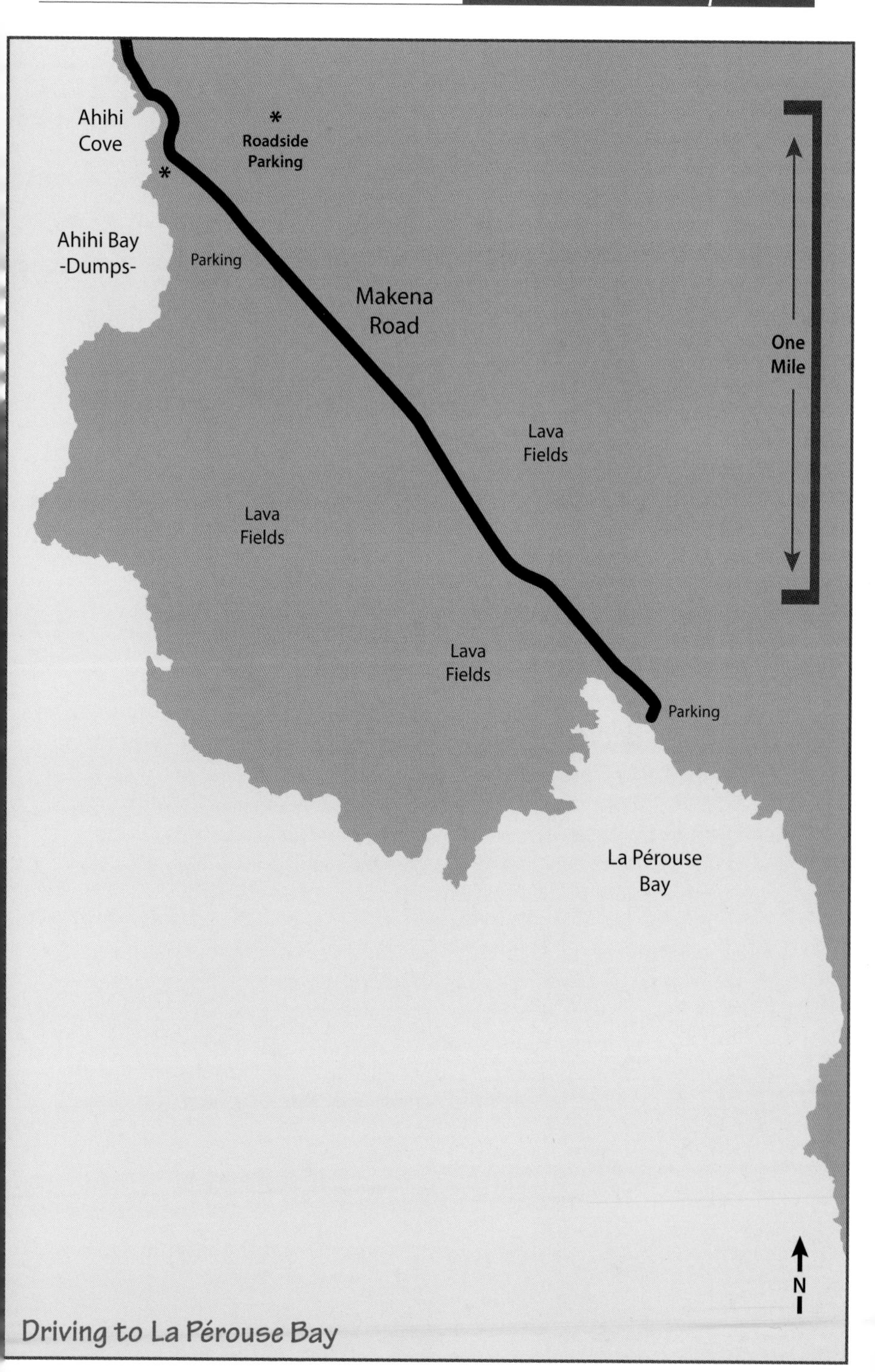
Ahihi
Cove
*
Roadside
Parking
*
Ahihi Bay
-Dumps-
Parking
Makena
Road
One
Mile
Lava
Fields
Lava
Fields
Lava
Fields
Parking
La Pérouse
Bay
N
Driving to La Pérouse Bay

Kamaʻole Beach I

Let's be honest, upon first encounter, Kihei can seem too busy, too crowded, too noisy, and a bit unsightly. It's not the picture you find on the postcard. But I'll tell you what, if you spend much time here, it'll grow on you and you're certain to discover its hidden charms. Among them is that steps from the hustle and bustle are some very beautiful beaches. A few of the best are the Kamaʻole Beaches in south Kihei. They are easy to access, have plenty of parking, and offer decent snorkeling.

The best snorkeling along the stretch of Kamaʻole Beaches is found at Kam I, with points off each end providing something to see. The south side has 300 yards of arched rocky shoreline to explore. It's an easy tune-up snorkel or a great training ground for those just getting their sea legs. Off the north end there's another 300 yard stretch to snorkel, with the added benefit of interesting coves and jumbles of rock strewn along the way. You'll find decent numbers of fish, pretty coral, and reasonably clear water.

Facilities: Showers and restrooms, shops and restaurants steps away.

Snorkeling: Entry for the north section is from the sand just before

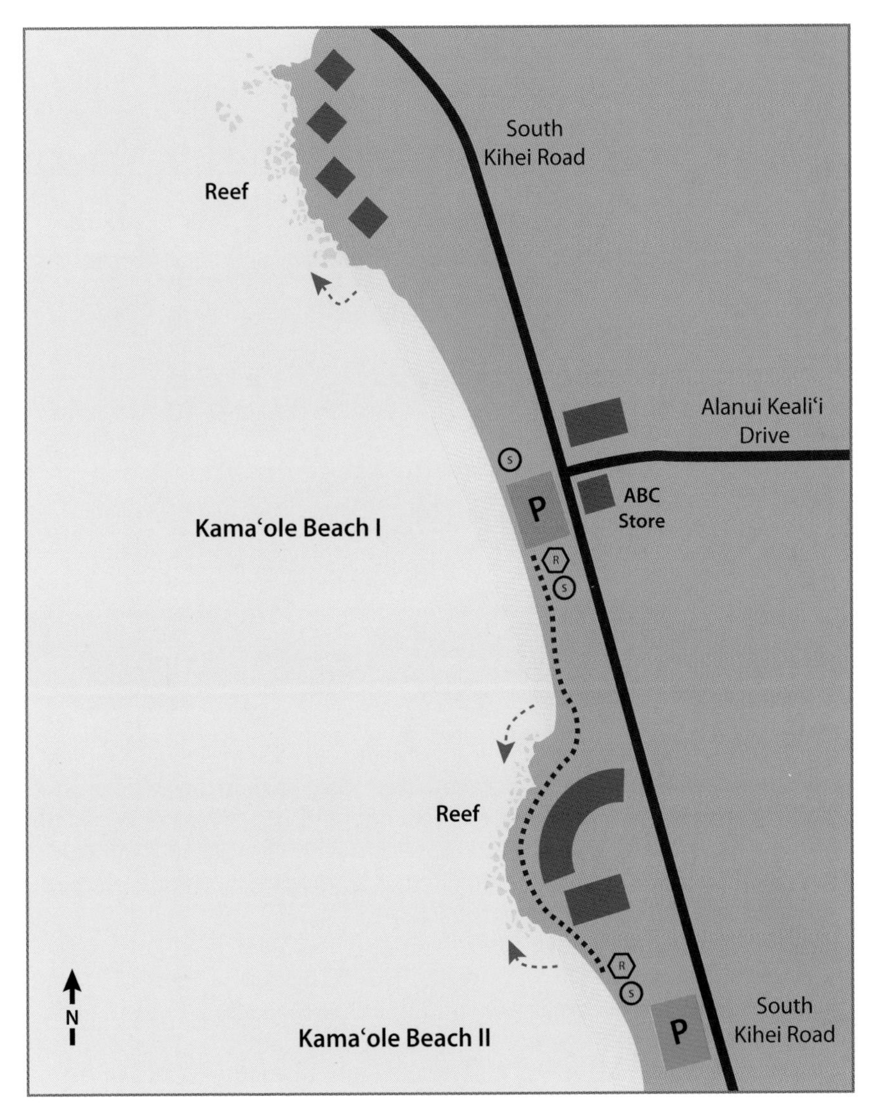

the start of the rocks. The water can be a little cloudy but usually clears as you swim out and northward. After about 80 yards, you'll notice the shoreline rocks opening into various small coves. If the depth is right and you're not fighting surge, check them out. The further you go the more interesting these shoreline coves become with a variety of fish and sea life. While cruising through here I once came upon a huge Stripebelly Pufferfish. These unique looking fish are fun to see.

Stripebelly Pufferfish

Surprisingly their skin and internal organs make them one of the most poisonous fish in the world. But you don't need to swim away if you see one—just don't plan an making a meal out of it! At the far north end of this stretch, you'll come to a twisting finger of rocks reaching out from shore. Rounding it brings you to Charlie Young Beach, a good place to turn around and make your way back.

The south end of Kam I offers an easy sand entry and shoreline swim. Snorkeling all the way around will bring you to Kam II. If the water is cloudy or becomes rough, there's a path on shore to walk back.

Location: South Maui, S. Kihei Road, south of Alanui Keali'i Drive.

From Hwy 30, turn toward the ocean on Alanui Keali'i Drive (2 miles south of Safeway). Follow Alanui Keali'i to South Kihei Road. Kam I is located just across the street.

From Wailea, follow Wailea-Alanui Road north to Okolani Drive. Turn left and follow Okolani to South Kihei Road. At just over 1½ miles you'll see an ABC store on the right. Parking for Kam I is just a few yards further on your left.

Kihei, Maui

Keawakapu Beach

When it comes to snorkeling, Keawakapu Beach is often overlooked. It shouldn't be and it's one of my personal favorites. It's easy to get to, fairly uncrowded, and offers decent numbers of fish and nice coral. The beach has two distinctly different snorkel areas separated by a half-mile stretch of sand. The south end is more of a traditional scramble of lava rocks that extends into the water providing pockets of coral and fish at various depths. It's not a huge area, but it's in good shape with a diverse population of life. The north end is similar but gives way to a lava rock wall that runs about 200 yards and opens to a deeper area of boulders and coral heads.

If you're staying in one of the condos along here, don't skip this beach. If you're driving, it's still worth a stop. You'll find plenty of parking with three different lots nearby. The one downside to this particular beach is its lack of bathrooms, with just one portable restroom located at the south parking area. Thankfully, there are showers at the central and south beach access points. Come early, because the water gets rough once the midday winds start blowing.

Facilities: Showers and one portable restroom on the south end.

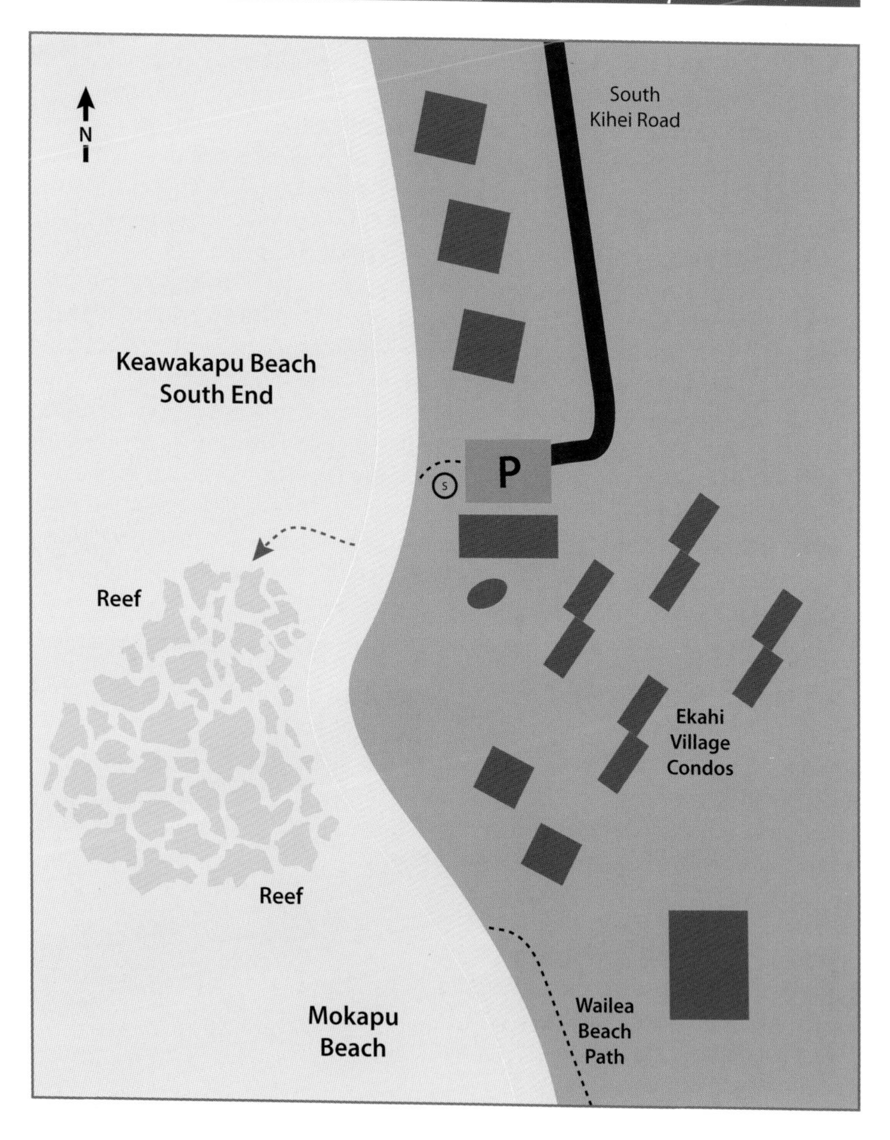

Snorkeling: Snorkeling the south end is about as straight forward as it gets. Enter the water from the sand near the rocks and follow the reef. Your biggest concern will be surge. There are a lot of shallow pockets that tempt exploration. If you cruise into one make sure you can get back out without smashing into the rocks or kicking the coral. Take your time. You're bound to see something interesting. I once came upon an octopus here—very cool. Water clarity always seems a little cloudier on the south side of this reef and gets worse as the day progresses.

Entry at the north end of the beach is much like the south and offers similar sights initially, but the edge of the reef is more defined and extends into deeper water. The shallow pockets are also more difficult to access comfortably—they get very shallow, so take extra care. I got banged up pretty good here when I misjudged the surge.

I've frequently found eels along the outer fringe of the reef no more than 40 yards out. I once saw a Whitemouth Moray cooperatively hunting with a Peacock Grouper. It's a fascinating behavior to watch. The fish and the eel work in tandem to flush prey from various hiding spots. They often touch noses before they start to hunt, then swim to a hole with the moray entering and the Peacock Grouper covering the exit. Watch for it, it's amazing to see. Sometimes you'll find a disinterested moray being prodded on by a grouper. It resembles harassment and I initially thought it was aggressive behavior by the grouper. John Hoover's "Ultimate Guide to Hawaiian Reef Fishes" set me straight. It's a great book, I highly recommend it.

Peacock Grouper and White Mouth Moray cooperatively hunting

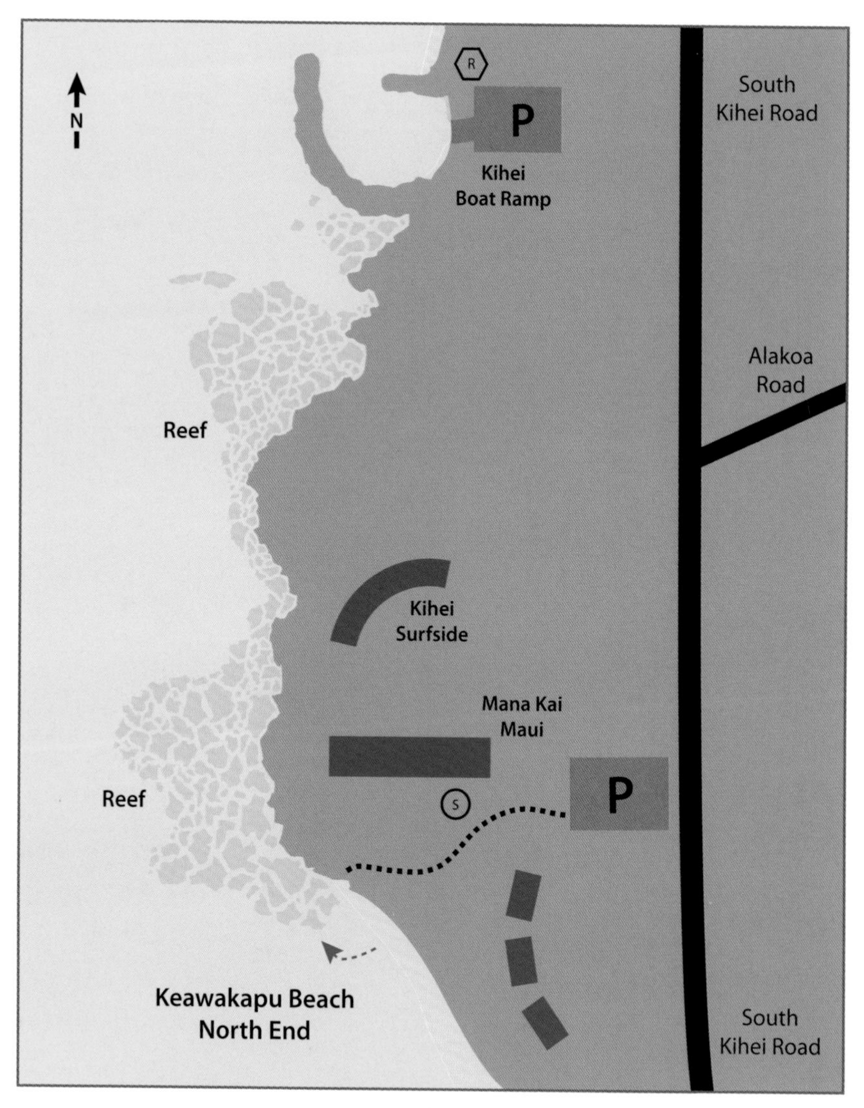

As you explore the reef north, you'll find it drops sharply to a sandy bottom and continues as a wall for about a hundred yards. It's often murky through here, but clears some as it opens to deeper water with boulders and coral heads. The next hundred yards offers a wide snorkeling area that extends to the jetty off the Kihei boat ramp, and serves as a good spot for turning around and heading back. There can be sizeable fish here but try not to venture beyond 75 yards from shore.

Much further will take you out of any worthwhile scenery and into potential boat traffic. Remember, you can see boats a lot better than they can see you.

Location: South Maui, South Kihei Road, between Kihei and Wailea.

From the Shops of Wailea, follow Wailea Alanui Road north to Okolani Drive. Turn left and follow Okolani to South Kihei Road. Depending on which part of the beach you want to visit, you have a choice between three parking areas:

The south parking lot is located at the southern end of South Kihei Road. Parking is limited. The middle parking lot is located on the south-east side of the intersection with Kilohana Drive. The north parking lot is located 80 yards south of the Mana Kai Resort.

Saddle Wrasse and Day Octopus

Ulua Beach

Ulua is a perfect place to learn to snorkel. It's a classic Maui beach with a beautiful crescent of sand, backed by coconut palms, stately monkeypod trees, and the lush manicured grounds of the condos above. It offers showers and bathrooms, and access to the Wailea Beach Path that winds its way along the shores of South Maui. Even if you don't want to snorkel, it's a great place to play in the water, watch the sunset, or just hang out. If it gets too crowded, Mokapu Beach is just steps away and can be deserted at sunset. It's hard to beat listening to waves and watching the sky turn to twilight in the evening here.

Snorkeling around this reef can get a little crowded. It has a gentle and protected entry that is popular for kids and beginners. If you have either in your party, be sure to bring them here, it's a comfortable place for an introduction to snorkeling. While Ulua's water clarity isn't always the best, there are reasonable numbers of fish, a large reef to explore and a variety of healthy corals that add to the underwater scenery.

For advanced snorkelers, come early in the day and you can avoid the majority of the crowds. The early morning usually offers better conditions with calmer, clearer water. Late afternoon tends to be choppy, but is often deserted. Let your judgment be your guide, but take care in the shallow areas over the reef.

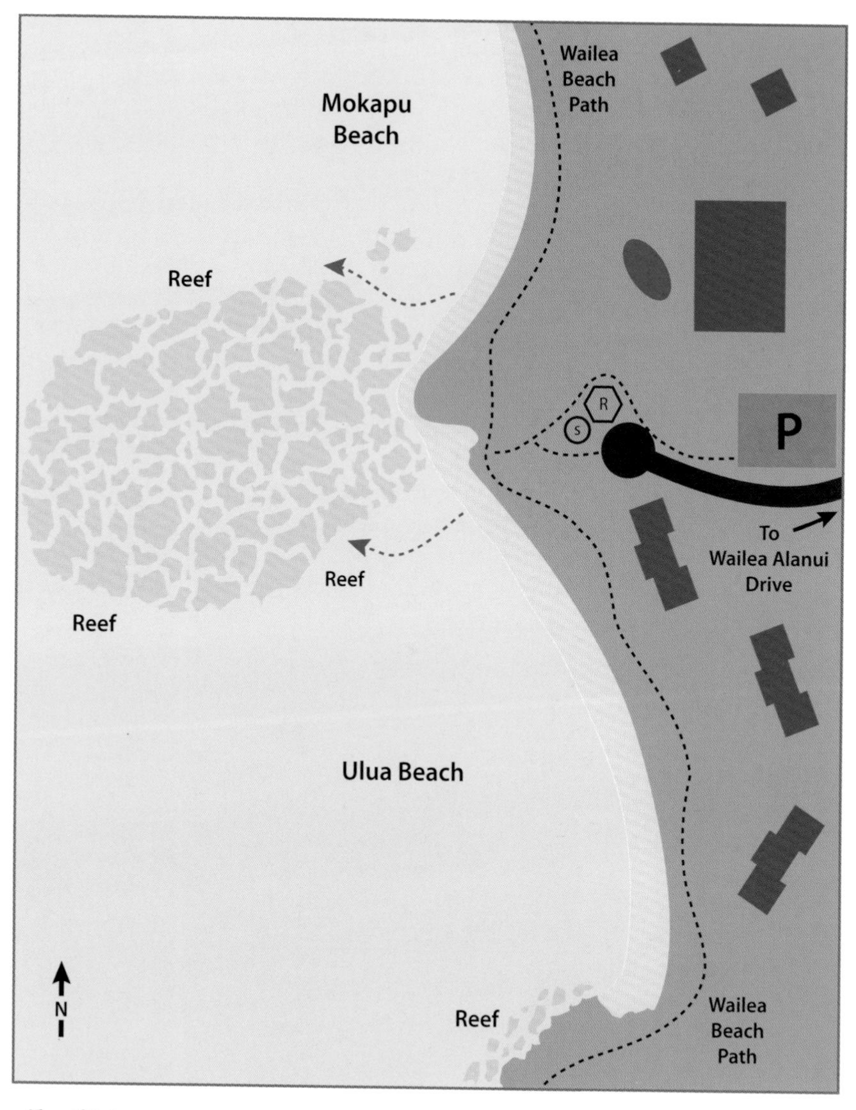

Facilities: Restrooms and showers.

Snorkeling: Enter from the sand a few yards south of the rocks and follow the reef out toward sea. The edge of the reef becomes an abrupt shelf as you move to deeper water and drops off to a sandy bottom. It's an easy guide for beginners to follow.

Advanced snorkelers may want to enter the water 30 yards from the rocks, swim out in an arc around the bulk of snorkelers, and make their way toward the further end of the reef. At the reef's far edge, it drops off into considerably deeper water and you'll often see scuba divers cruising along the bottom 25 feet below. This is where you'll find larger fish and possibly a turtle. It's fun to dive down along this edge and search the overhanging areas for hidden creatures.

In the shallower waters above the reef, you can follow a maze of paths through the coral. Take your time, it's an interesting spot to explore. You're likely to see large boxfish, eels, or an octopus along the way. Once while snorkeling Ulua, we saw an octopus traveling about the reef. As it moved through the water its texture was as streamlined as a bullet, but within seconds of stopping its skin would bump, bulge, thicken, and change color until we swore we were looking at a rock. It was an incredible feat of camouflage—count yourself lucky if you're ever treated to a performance.

For those who want to continue around the point, it's an easy snorkel over to Mokapu Beach. Unfortunately, water clarity often suffers on this side, and if it's too cloudy it can be difficult to follow the rocks without threat of running into them. If you find yourself in a murky spot, arc away from the rocks and swim to shore.

Ulua Reef

Day Octopus - Ulua Reef

Location: South Maui, Wailea Alanui Road, a quarter-mile north of the Shops of Wailea.

From the Shops of Wailea, follow Wailea Alanui Road north and look for Ulua Beach signs. The cross street is Hale Ali'i Place.

Wailea Beach

To call this beach a popular spot would be an understatement. Wailea has been ranked as one of America's best beaches several times and needless to say, it can get crowded. Its long swath of inviting sand is bordered by lava bluffs at each end and backed by the lush tropical foliage of the Grand Wailea and Four Seasons Resort. It's a beautiful setting and a fun place to play in the water, snorkel, and relax. Wailea is a "full service beach" with restrooms and showers, resort restaurants, and rental services with just about everything you need for a day at the beach: snorkel gear, kayaks, paddle and boogie boards, as well as lounge chairs and umbrellas. To top it all off you can take a stroll along Wailea's scenic beach path, or kick back and dry out after a long snorkel under the shade of palm trees on the grassy hill just above the beach.

The snorkeling here is very good but is condition dependent. To do it right, you need to get here early before the waves pick up and the snorkel boats load the water with customers. Wailea Beach is another spot where you're able to access snorkel areas for free that others are paying $70 or more to visit. How great is that?

The area has nice coral, decent fish counts, turtles, and some cool pockets of mini-coves along the lava rock shoreline. You'll want to spend most of your snorkel time off the south end of the beach.

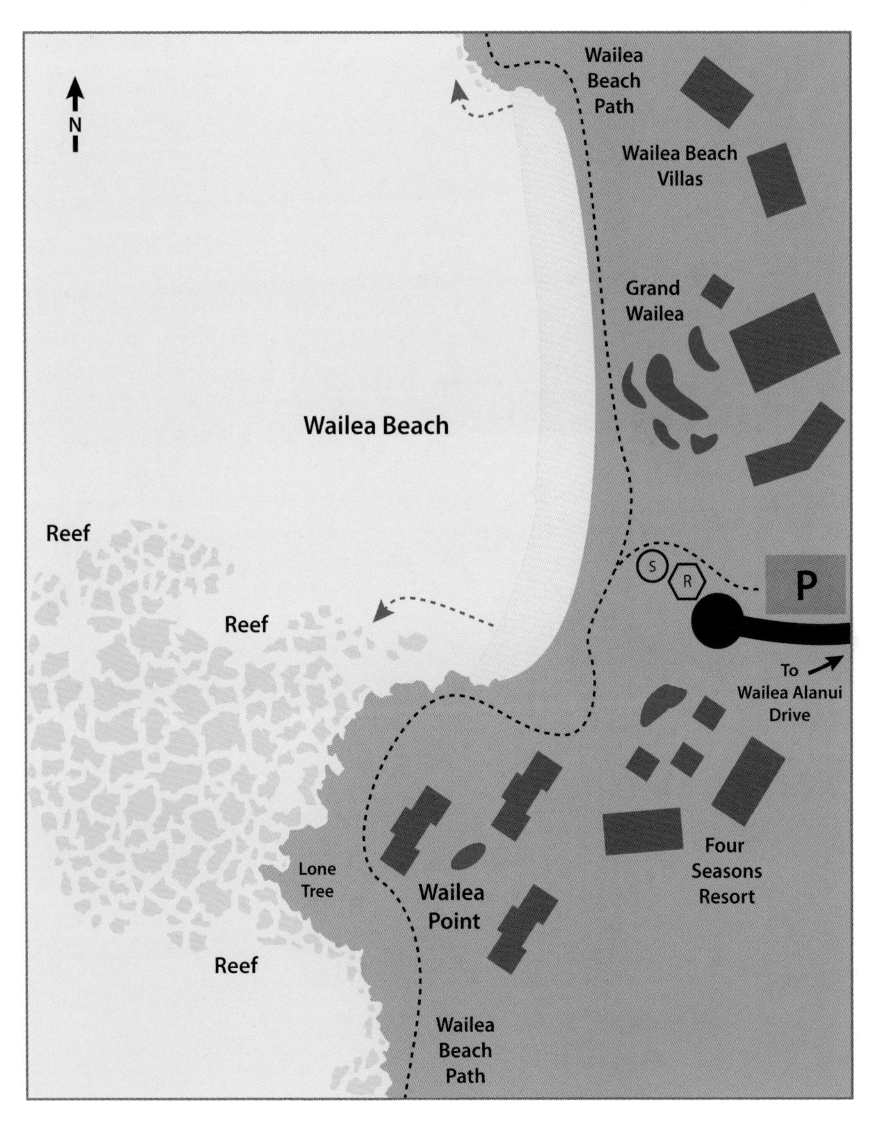

Facilities: Restrooms and showers. Gear rental on the beach.

Snorkeling: It's best to enter the water from the sand several yards before reaching the rocks. Then swim out past the breakers, angle over toward the rocks, and follow them out. About 100 yards from shore you'll reach the point and start getting into some nice coral and fish. The reef extends out and continues south around the point for several hundred yards. It's a large area with a lot to explore. About 150 yards south,

you'll see a lone tree on the shoreline. Just off this tree is a spot that's popular with the snorkel boats. If you're interested in exploring the area, hit it early so you're ready to move on when the mass of humanity arrives—it can get seriously crowded!

The lava rock shoreline is a neat place to explore. Arms of lava stretch into the sea and create numerous pockets of water that often attract a number of good-sized fish. If you haven't seen any turtles, this is the place to look. They frequently come here to eat algae off the rocks. Enjoy their presence but please give them space and let them go about their business. Turtles are pretty mellow and will generally hang around if they're not harassed.

If large waves start kicking up, this whole area loses its attraction. The reef can still be snorkeled, but it's not a lot of fun. You'll be tossed

Snorkel boat off Wailea Reef

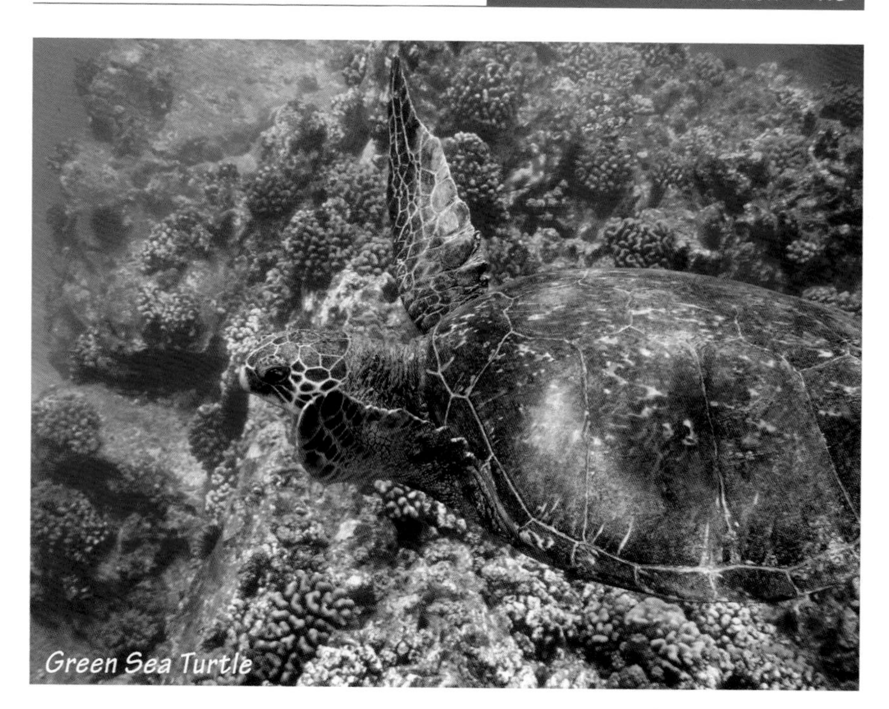
Green Sea Turtle

endlessly. As far as the shoreline rocks, they're a total no-go. Getting smashed into lava is not anyone's idea of a favorite vacation memory.

For a longer snorkel excursion, round the point, check out the near-shore rock area, then meander out through the coral heading south for 100 yards or so. Once you've had your fill, swim back toward the shoreline rocks and follow them south, exiting at Polo Beach. Depending on how much backtracking you do, you'll cover between half to three-quarters of a mile. The walk back along the beach path is an added bonus providing an elevated view of your snorkel path. It's barefoot-friendly and about half-mile trek to Wailea Beach.

Location: South Maui, Wailea Alanui Road, south of the Grand Wailea.

From Wailea, follow Wailea Alanui Road south to the Grand Wailea. Just beyond the resort entrance the road will begin to climb. Look for a sign on the right for beach parking.

Polo Beach

Polo Beach is a pretty spot and a nice place to spend the day, but it's definitely not a snorkel destination. Located just below the Fairmont Kea Lani, its 300 yards of sandy shores are best enjoyed sunning on the beach, playing in the water, and appreciating the beautiful setting. That said, if you have your gear and want to check things out, the lava rocks that border each end provide your best bet for exploration—just keep your expectations low. While snorkeling opportunities are limited, it's an easy place to visit with ample parking, restrooms, and showers.

Depending on the direction you're headed, Polo Beach also marks the starting or ending point for the Wailea Beach Path that meanders along some of the most scenic shoreline of South Maui. Walking the full length of the path is about three miles round-trip and provides a great way to get to know the area. You can check out the resorts, see the beaches and enjoy fantastic views at nearly every turn.

Facilities: Restrooms and showers. Access to Wailea Beach Path.

Snorkeling: On the south end of the beach a broken jumble of lava forms a rocky point stretching into the water. You'll find a small amount of coral and may encounter a few fish. It's shallow so put some distance

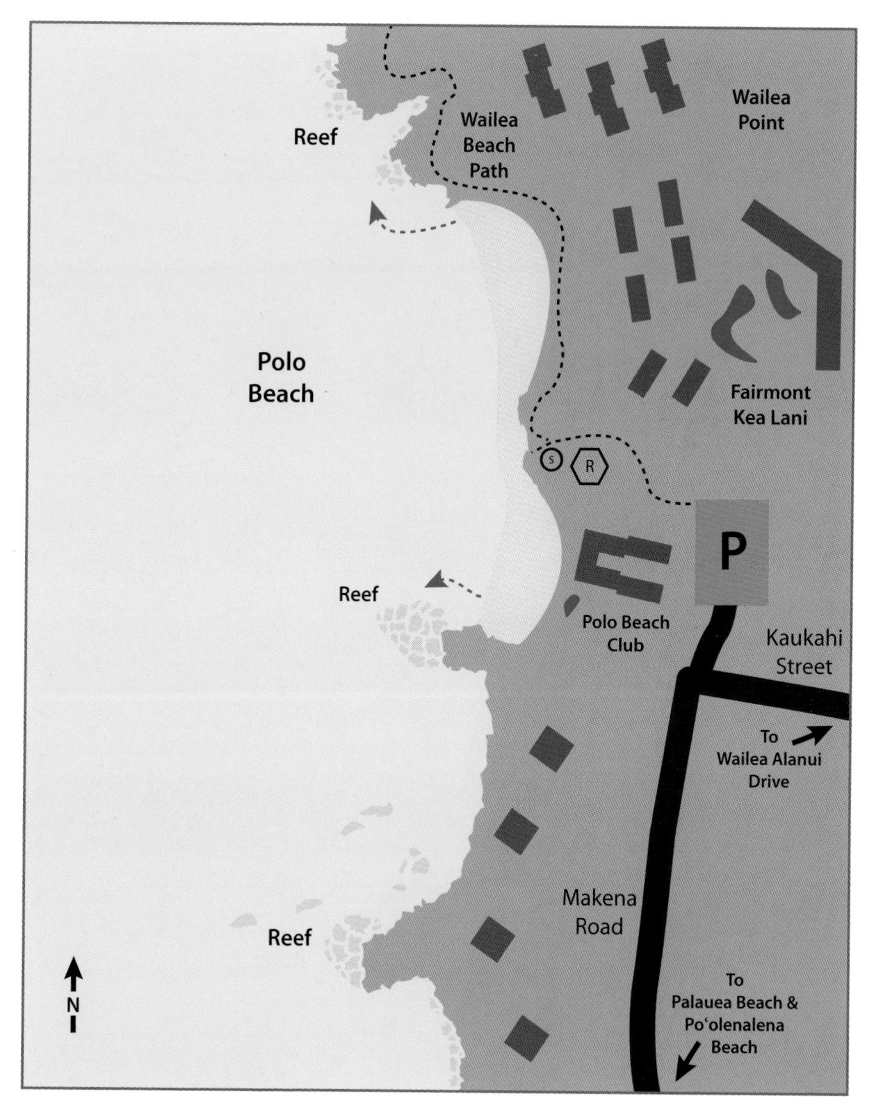

between yourself and the rocks as you're entering. Snorkeling around the point will bring you into a small cove. It's often cloudy and fairly unremarkable, though I once ran into a group of Great Barracudas close to shore—very cool!

The north side of the beach is the start of a lava rock bluff that winds its way to Wailea Beach. Craggy fingers of rock reach into the water for a half-mile of shoreline and provide a multitude of mini coves and fissures. It's an unusual area and offers a unique snorkel. It's also a great

Great Barracuda

place to see turtles. They like to come here and eat the algae that drape the rocks. If the water is calm, you can have quite an expedition snorkeling to Wailea Point, exploring the reef, and heading back to Polo along the beach path. It's a nice walk back, easy on bare feet, and provides a scenic view of your excursion.

Only snorkel the north section if the water is calm. If the waves are crashing you can't get close enough to the rocks to see anything without some serious risk.

Location: South Maui, Makena Road, about 1¼ mile south of Wailea.

From Wailea, drive south on Wailea Alanui Road for about one mile. Take a right on Kaukahi, just past the Kea Lani. Proceed on Kaukahi and take a right on Makena Road. Follow the signs for beach parking.

Wailea Beach Path

Palauea Beach

What a spot! Palauea is a beautiful sand beach backed by tropical vegetation with good snorkeling, and easy access. You'd expect it to be teeming with people, but lacking resorts and condos it's much less visited and rare to find crowds of snorkelers here. Parking is along the road with trails leading through the trees to the beach.

The south end provides your best bet for allocating your time, but decent snorkeling can be found on the north end as well. You'll find healthy coral and respectable numbers of fish, though water clarity can be a bit of a mixed bag. If you decide to snorkel here it's best to have a flexible plan. If the water is cloudy, just head to another spot. Makena Landing and Maluaka are close and both offer great snorkeling.

Facilities: Portable restrooms, no showers.

Snorkeling: Enter the water on the south side of the beach about 20 yards before the sand ends. Swim out a bit and make your way over toward the rocks. As you move away from the beach, the water should clear. If it's calm enough, cruise along the rocks exploring the pockets of coral. It's often a good place to find eels.

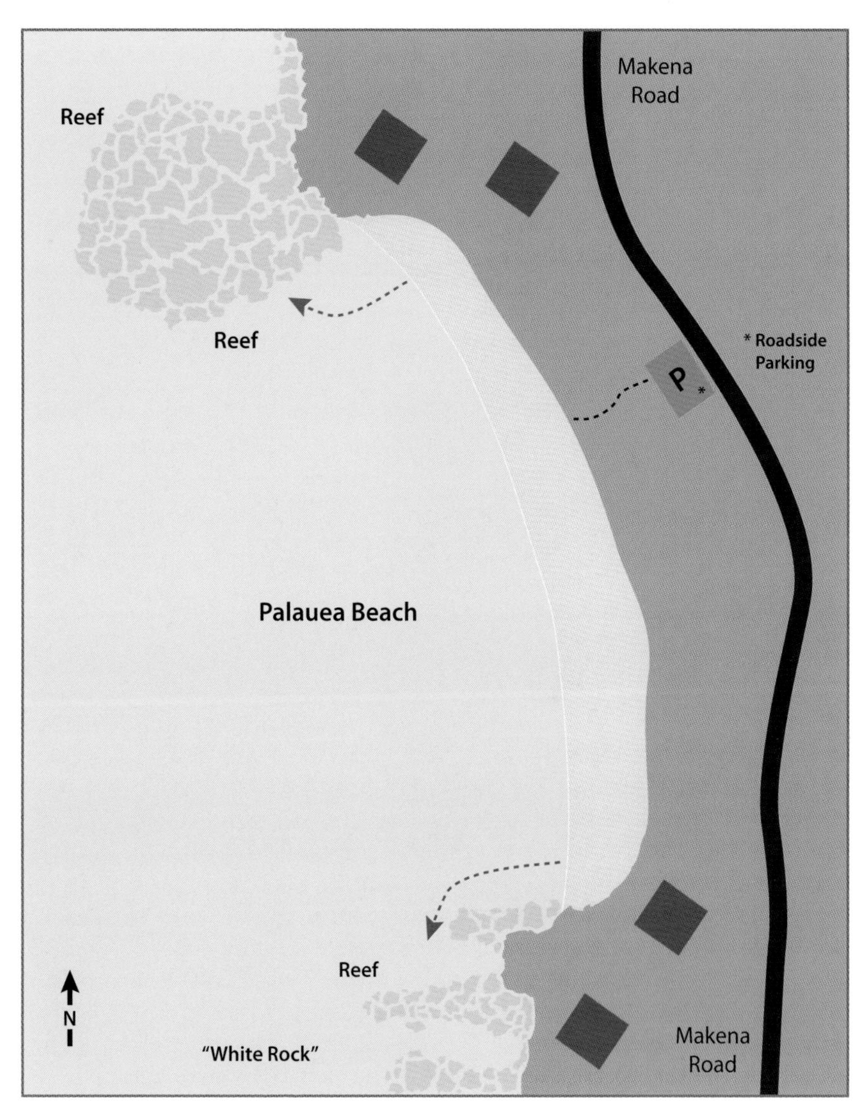

The area extends further south for a few hundred yards and is punctuated with lava rock arms that extend out from shore and break the surface now and again. This part of the reef is often referred to as White Rock. If the water is clear, be sure to explore the whole area. Swimming all the way around the far south point will bring you to a rocky shoreline that leads to the north end of Poʻolenalena Beach. It's a long journey, but if the conditions are right, you'll cover some beautiful territory. There's a small, hidden pocket of sand that's separated from the larger beach by rocks. You may very well have the spot to yourself. Round trip, it's about a three-quarter mile swim.

We were snorkeling off White Rock when we were fortunate enough to encounter five huge manta rays. What an incredible experience. With their enormous wingspan they'd be intimidating if you didn't know anything about them, but manta rays are gentle creatures. The day of our encounter the mantas were gracefully circling through the reef for over a half hour. Seeing those massive rays leisurely gliding by provided a snorkeling highlight we'll never forget.

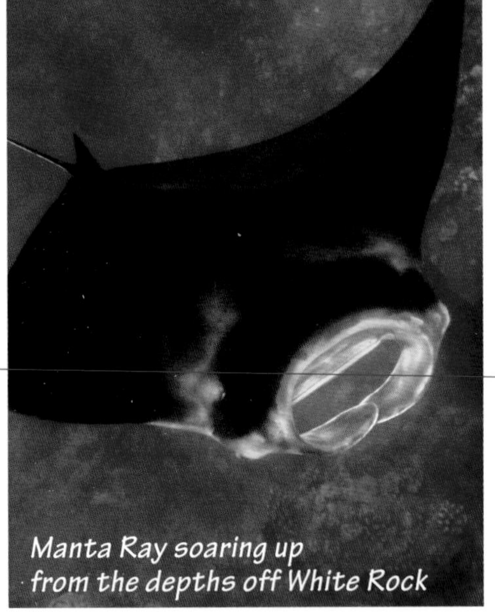
Manta Ray soaring up from the depths off White Rock

To snorkel the north end of Palauea, enter the water from the sand just before it meets the rocks. The shoreline curls out and around, so this entry should put you beyond the surf. Follow the rocks out toward sea. The area off the point can get shallow and extends close to a hundred yards. Further around the point are little "pocket coves" that dot the shoreline for about 50 yards. They're fun to explore, but take note of any surge and adjust your position accordingly.

If you're feeling particularly adventurous, around the far northern point is a shallow cove where I once came across a group of Great Barracudas. They're known for frequenting the same areas, so you never know, you just may encounter them yourself. This cove can also be accessed from the south end of Polo Beach.

Location: South Maui, Makena Road, about 1¼ mile south of Wailea.

From Wailea, drive one mile south on Wailea Alanui Road. Take a right on Kaukahi, just past the Kea Lani. Follow Kaukahi to Makena Road and take a left. At just over quarter-mile you'll see a stretch of trees with cars parked along the road—this is it. You'll see an established trail to the beach at the south end near the portable restrooms.

Whitemouth Moray

Moray Eels: Morays are pretty cool to see and one of my favorite underwater creatures to photograph. At first glance they can seem pretty intimidating. You'll often find them poking their snake-like heads out of dark crevices—opening and closing their jaws and displaying a mouthful of teeth in a threatening manner. No need to rush off if you see one though, morays aren't typically aggressive unless they're being harassed or fed. While they may not look like it, eels are actually fish. But unlike fish, moray eels don't have gill covers. This makes a big difference when it comes to breathing. Fish breathe by opening and closing their gill covers to draw water across their gills, while morays have to constantly open and close their mouths to do the same thing. So while they may look menacing, morays are just doing "what morays have to do" in order to breathe. Eels also make great subjects to photograph. Their tendency to stay in one place makes getting a good shot a little easier than other sea creatures. But if you're lucky enough to watch an eel hunt, be prepared for a challenge, they can move fast when they want!

Po'olenalena Beach

Po'olenalena is a nice beach with a lot to offer. From the Makena Surf Condos its sandy shoreline stretches north for over a half-mile. You'll find rocky points with great snorkeling on each side, a few shade trees, and a very tan local guy sporting a thong and a guitar offering up songs to the morning. One way or another, the place is guaranteed to put a smile on your face.

While separated by a half-mile of sand, the snorkeling is good on both ends with seemingly higher fish counts on the north end. If the water is clear, save enough time and energy to check out both sides. Parking is available in two places: a small paved lot to the south and a larger gravel lot midway down the beach.

The south end starts where the sand meets the rocks in front of the Makena Surf Condos (see map, p. 127). The whole area from here around the point to Chang's Beach offers plenty to see. Water clarity and fish counts may be spotty, but often improve over a short distance. Turtles are common. If you plan to start on the south end, arrive early so you can park in the small public lot in front of the condos. It's a lot closer to your entry and shortens the walk when you're carrying gear.

Snorkeling the north end requires a bit of a hike. You'll want to park in the gravel lot, take the beach trail to the north skirting the lava rocks,

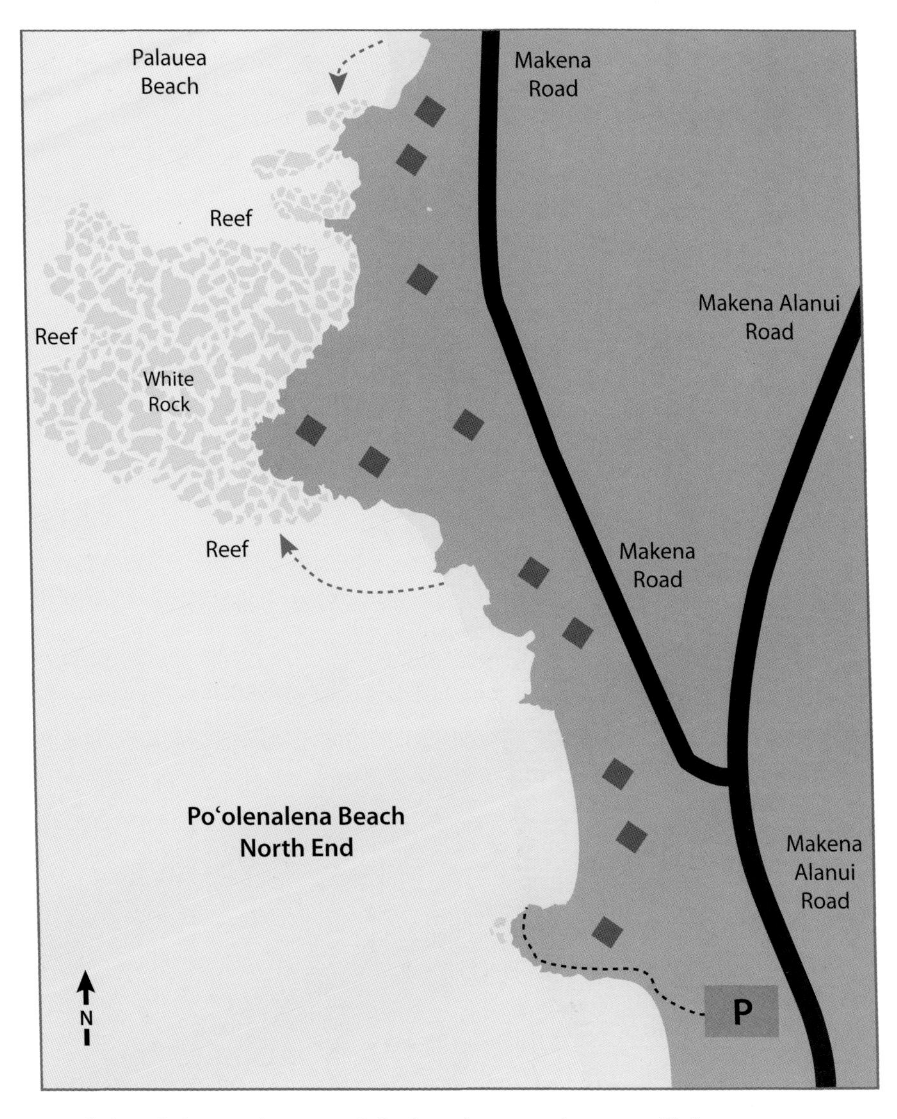

and then hike up the rest of the beach. From here you'll do some swimming before seeing anything worthwhile. Often referred to as White Rock, this area makes you work, but can be worth the effort. It was off this point we encountered a group of five Manta Rays.

Facilities: Portable restrooms are located at the north end of the beach near the gravel parking area. Showers can be found on the south end of the beach just below Makena Surf Condos.

Snorkeling: The south end entry is pretty straightforward. Enter the water about ten yards before the lava rocks and swim in an arc toward the outer rock point (see map, p. 127). The water can be particularly turbid the closer to the beach you are and will clear considerably as you proceed. You'll want to follow this rocky shoreline out and around for the best snorkeling. As you swim around the point you'll find pockets of deeper water and likely see a turtle or two. The further you swim the better the coral becomes. On the very far side is some of the nicest coral on the island. It can be cloudy here, but when it's clear it's incredibly beautiful. It gets shallow in spots, so be careful not to kick the coral. Also take note of the surge, you don't want to get tossed onto the rocks. Once around the point, the small beach tucked into the shoreline is Chang's Beach. It's a nice spot to take a break before swimming back to Po'olenalena.

The north end is also a sand entry, but requires a tenth of a mile swim before you get to the reef and coral. Hike to the end of the beach and enter the water about thirty yards before the rocks. Swim straight out another thirty yards, then angle your direction so you'll intersect the rocky shoreline at its mid-point. The closer to the beach you are the cloudier the water will be, and sometimes it's just murky no matter what. Follow the rocks to the point and into deeper water.

Green Sea Turtle

You'll encounter shelves at varying depths that you can dive down and explore. Thirty yards out from the point and below the surface is an elevated spire of lava rock. Just off this spot is where we encountered the manta rays. I'll readily admit to being spooked when a huge dark shape arose from the depths. But my unease was swiftly replaced with amazement when I realized it was a manta ray followed by four more—what a sight!

Pencil urchins and coral

If you swim back toward shore and continue around the point you'll encounter a long stretch of rocky shoreline with interesting pockets to scout. About ninety yards along, rocky points occasionally break the surface extending out from the shore. When clarity is good, this can be another interesting place to explore. Known as White Rock this area can also be accessed from Palauea Beach to the north. If you're up for it and conditions are right, snorkeling all the way around can be great, and the beach provides a nice resting place before swimming back. Hiking is an option, but at just over a half-mile it can be a little rough on bare feet.

Location: South Maui, Makena Alanui Road, 1 ¾ miles south of Wailea.

From Wailea, drive 1 ¾ miles south on Wailea Alanui Road/Makena Alanui Road. The first public parking area is just past Makena Road on your right. The second is a small lot a little further down the road in front of Makena Surf Condos.

Chang's Beach

Chang's Beach is an overlooked spot that sees little pressure compared to the better-known snorkel spots. As a result, the coral is in fantastic shape. Unfortunately, water clarity can be an issue. Sometimes it's clear, other times it's completely blown out. Since Chang's is an easy place to visit, adding a stop on your way to another snorkel spot is a great way to sample the water without investing a lot of time. If things are clear, you can snorkel to your heart's content. If it's murky, you can head elsewhere without burning much of your day or simply enjoy the sun and surf from the sand of this pretty little beach.

The beach provides a pocket of sand nestled between two rocky outcroppings. It's backed by an elevated shoreline with the Makena Surf Condos on one end and private residences on the other. If you didn't know any better, you might think it's a private beach. But like all of Maui, the beaches are public and you're welcome to enjoy it. The best snorkeling is off the point on the right side and entry is from the sand. Fish presence can be a mixed bag, but turtles are common and the coral is beautiful. If you take your time you're sure to find plenty to enjoy.

Facilities: None. Showers and restrooms are available a half-mile south at Makena Beach Park on Makena Road.

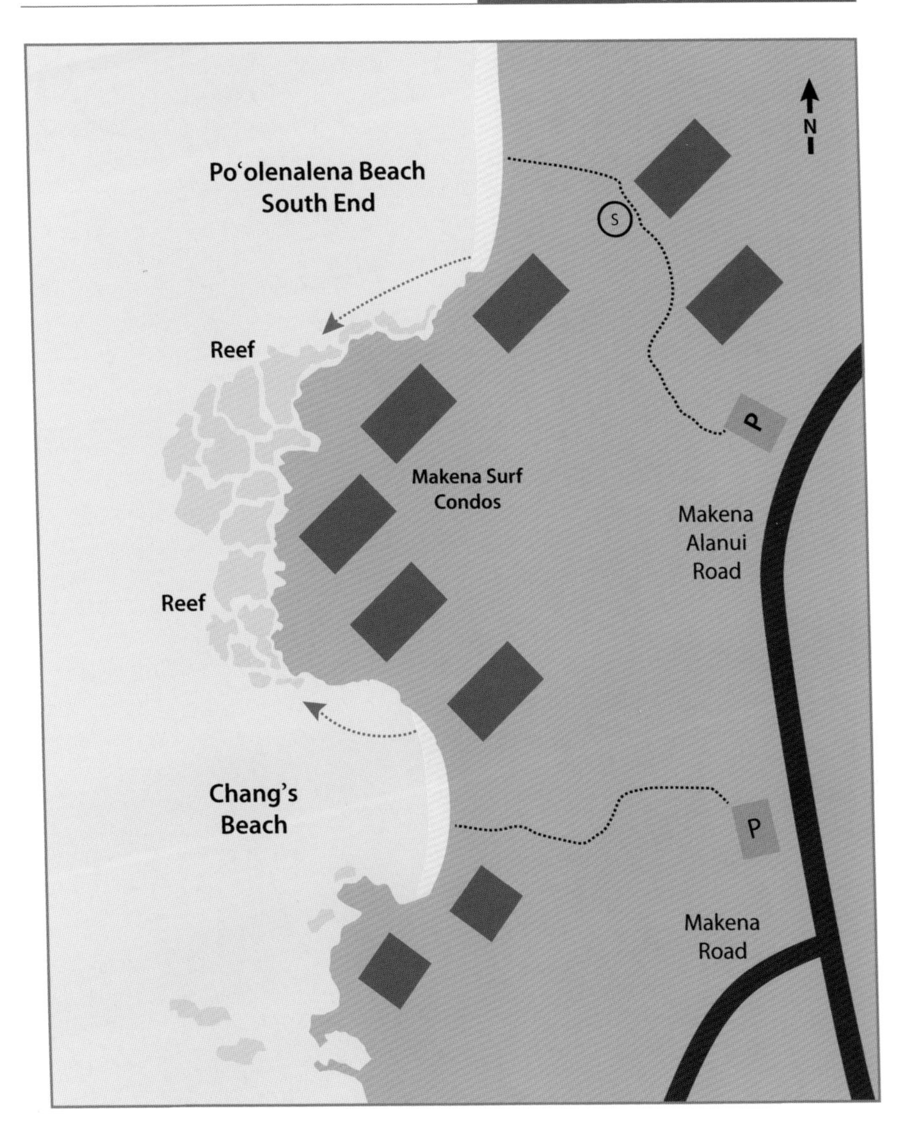

Snorkeling: Entry doesn't get much easier. Just wade in from the sand and head out in either direction. The rocks on both ends of the beach provide something to see, but the point off the right side hosts lots of healthy coral dotted with bright red pencil urchins. Between the two points is a sandy expanse that leads up to the beach.

Snorkeling the right side, the water depth will drop quickly along the rocks. As you proceed, the depth will give way to ledges of coral encrusted rock with some spots becoming very shallow. Watch for surge and take care not to kick the coral as you venture over these areas. If you take your time and look closely among the coral in these shallow spots you'll see tons of life on a miniature scale. As you swim over the deeper pockets go slow. A close inspection among the rocks may yield an octopus, eel, or turtles resting below.

Swimming further out and continuing to the right provides a wide expanse to explore. Water clarity can often vary from spot to spot and if you continue around the point, you'll eventually arrive at the southern end of Po'olenalena Beach. Exiting here will require a quarter-mile walk back to your vehicle. Let your curiosity and judgment be your guide.

Snorkeling the left side of Chang's, the rocks provide several small pockets of water to explore. In some of the deeper areas I've found groups of Bluespotted Cornetfish. With their elongated bodies and large blue spots, they're quite a sight to see. If you continue around the rocks, you'll arrive at a shallow cove that offers a great spot to see Needlefish. Swim slowly and scan the waterline. Large schools of these slender fish can be found just below the surface. When you've finished exploring the left side, you'll need to swim back to the beach. There's no shore access from this cove.

Arc-Eye Hawkfish, Cauliflower Coral, and Pencil Urchin

Turtle Cleaning - Chang's Beach

Location: South Maui, Makena Alanui Road, 2 miles south of Wailea.

From Wailea, drive 2 miles south on Wailea Alanui Road/Makena Alanui Road to the Makena Surf Condos, look for them on your right. There are two small public parking lots. The first provides access to the south end of Poʻolenalena. The second is for Chang's Beach. Take note, these lots are easy to miss and fill up quickly. From the parking lot, follow the path to the beach.

Five Caves - Five Graves

Named for its sea caves and nearby grave sites, the snorkeling at Five Caves - Five Graves is as intriguing as its name. While entry is a pain and conditions can be a challenge, it's an awesome spot and one of my favorites. If I have plenty of time, I like to access the area from Makena Landing and have a marathon adventure all the way to Chang's Beach. If you don't have two hours to spend and just want to get to the heart of the area's best snorkeling, this is the place to put in.

The snorkeling offers good fish counts, great coral, and awe-inspiring caverns, arches, and crevices. It's a little deeper than many snorkel areas, with depths exceeding 40 feet. But it's also variable—some spots over a hundred yards from shore may only be 8 feet deep. In any case, the marine life and variety of scenery offers plenty to explore.

Sometimes paid snorkel tours anchor their boats off the outer edge of the reef and it can get pretty busy. If you prefer solitude, a few quick fin kicks can take you to areas where the tours can't follow. Enjoy the freedom, it's another benefit of having shoreline access.

There are no facilities here. Parking is on the east side of the road and a short path leads to the water. You'll pass a small plot of land that is host to the namesake, Five Graves. Walking distance is less than 150 yards. Entry is from the rocks at the end of a narrow, channel-like cove.

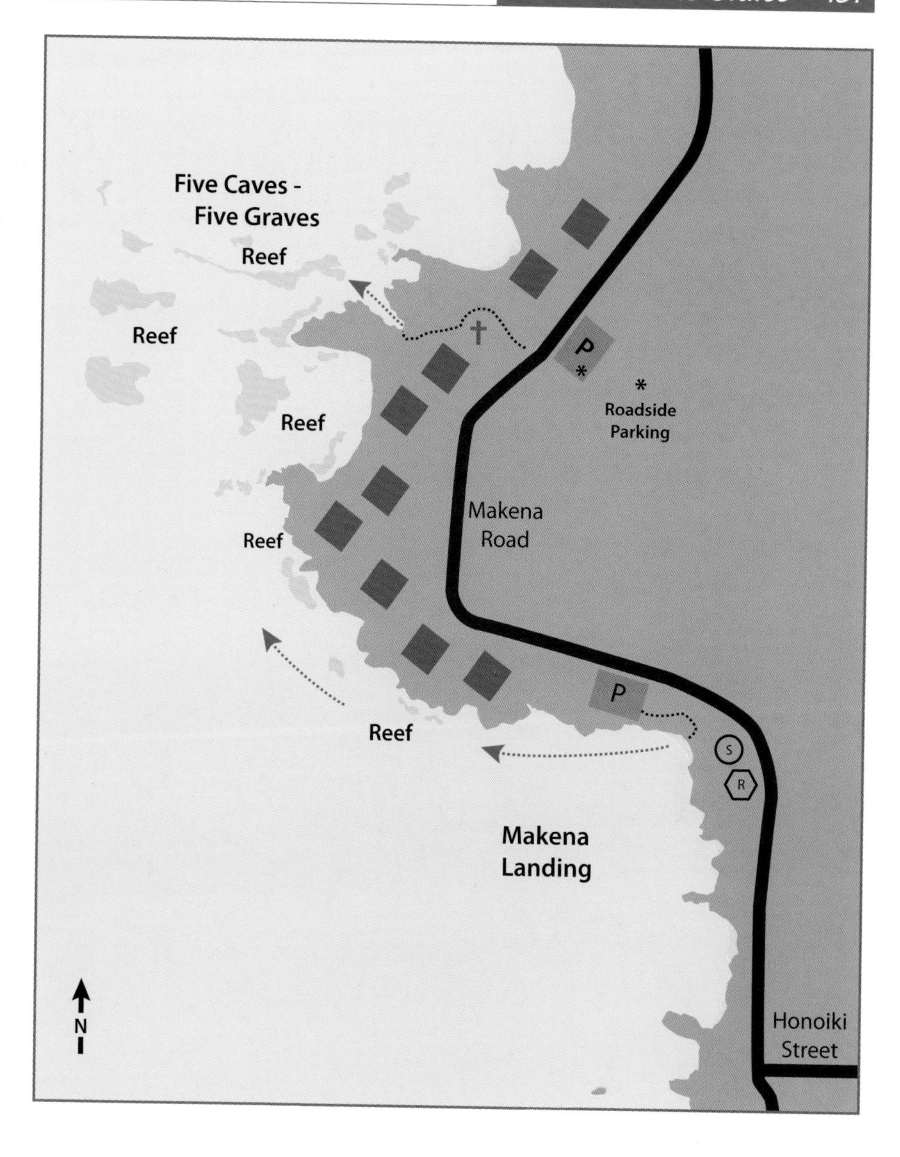

Facilities: None. Makena Landing offers showers and restrooms a quarter-mile to the south.

Snorkeling: Entry can be tricky and you'll want to ready your gear, position yourself, and work with the waves. If you linger in the shallows, you can get tumbled back onto the rocks. They host a few urchins, so take care. I like to enter just after a wave, slip on my mask, and kick out a few yards to deeper water, pulling on my fins as I go. Needless to say, unless it's calm, it's a spot better left to experienced snorkelers.

As you leave the cove you can head in either direction, but the best snorkeling is found to your left. Follow the ledge on its way out from shore and you'll enter some magnificent territory. The coral encrusted rock formations are amazing. Look closely for turtles as you swim over the various canyons, they're very common through here. If you dive down along the ledge you'll occasionally see cave-like pockets sheltering larger fish. You may even see a Whitetip Reef Shark. Give them plenty of room. While they're not known to be aggressive, there's no reason to push it.

When you reach the shoreline point at the end of the ledge, take notice of how it continues underwater. It extends another hundred yards and is worth following. The depth varies, dropping and rising along the way. You'll find lots of fish and plenty of beautiful coral. A hundred yards south and equally distant from shore provides yet another coral encrusted shelf rising from the depths and just as grand as the first. It's not a bad idea to explore this whole outer reef early and enjoy it before any snorkel tours arrive. Tour boats typically anchor close by and can unload quite a crowd. After snorkeling the outer reef be sure to take in

Green Sea Turtle

Convict Tangs

the area closer to shore between the two points. You'll find it loaded with more canyons, arches, and intriguing formations.

If you follow the shoreline south and around the corner, you'll find decent snorkeling much of the way eventually reaching Makena Landing. This popular park offers bathrooms and showers, and a quarter-mile hike north along Makena Road will get you back to your car. The best choice is to explore south a short distance around the corner, then turn around and snorkel back to the entry cove at Five Caves - Five Graves.

On the north side of the entry is an area of coral followed by three coves. The water clarity through here can vary considerably. My advice is to take a pass on the first cove and explore the points off the second. This cove can offer a good place to spot Needlefish just below the water's surface. The third cove brings you to Chang's Beach. The snorkeling on the north side of Chang's can be fantastic. Beautiful coral and sea turtles are often a regular part of the scenery. Its small sandy beach also provides an inviting spot to take a breather before swimming back to Five Caves - Five Graves. If you decide to get out at Chang's Beach, the hike back to your car is about a third of a mile.

The magnificent scenery of Five Caves - Five Graves

Location: South Maui, Makena Road, about 2¼ miles south of Wailea.

From Wailea, drive 2¼ miles south on Wailea Alanui Road/Makena Alanui Road to Makena Surf Condos. Just past the condos turn right on Makena Road. At about a third of a mile you'll see a pull-off for parking

on your left. The path to the entry cove is across the road adjacent to several old grave sites.

Makena Landing

Makena Landing is an all around great spot. While not a true beach, it's a jack-of-all-trades. It's popular for launching kayaks, playing in the water, sitting on the grass, or heading out for a scuba dive. In addition to bathrooms and showers, you'll find a decent amount of parking, shade trees, and a nice grassy area to relax after a long snorkel. Not to mention, the view of the South Maui shoreline is hard to beat.

The snorkeling in the immediate launch area isn't good, but if you're willing to swim a little, it's a gateway to some of Maui's best snorkeling. An ideal excursion involves setting out from here, rounding the point, exploring the outer reef, and following the ledge to Five Caves - Five Graves. You can then continue on to Chang's Beach, take a breather on the sand, and make the return trip. It's a marathon and should only be undertaken in calm conditions, but it's truly a fantastic outing.

Another great snorkeling option can be found by exploring an area just south of the park (see map, page 139). It's a hike or long swim before reaching anything worthwhile, but a vast treasure of beautiful coral hides just beyond an offshore jumble of lava rocks. Very few people venture here and conditions can make it unpredictable, but when it's calm and clear it can be a delight.

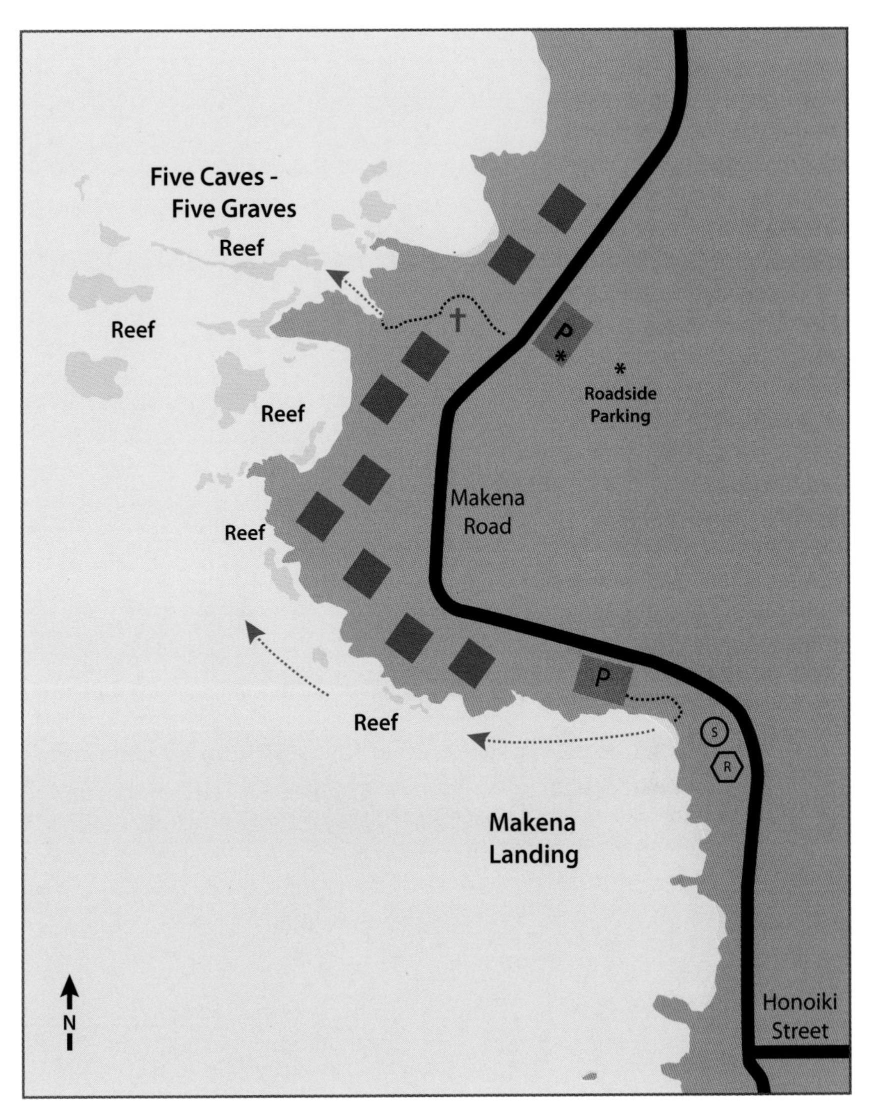

Water clarity at Makena Landing can be spotty. It's often poor in the immediate launch area, becoming clearer as you swim along the rocky shore on the right. Much of the snorkeling includes deeper water than many other locations and is loaded with canyons, arches, ledges, and underwater caves. A variety of fish of decent size and numbers inhabit the area, and turtles are a common sight. There's a lot to see here as evidenced by the numerous snorkel tours that drop anchor

Snorkel Boat Tour

nearby—though that's another sight altogether. I'm not sure what's more frightening to see: a shark fin coming your way or a horde of 50 snorkelers just off the boat. Thankfully there's a lot of territory to explore and unlike the snorkelers from the tour boats, you're free to roam.

Facilities: Restrooms and showers. Boat ramp and kayak launch.

Snorkeling: To snorkel the northern area, it's best to enter at the boat ramp by the restrooms. Simply wade in, gear up and go. An alternative entrance can be made from the rocks at the far end of the parking lot. It might save a little swim time, but the rocks can be slick and picking a safe and easy spot makes it tricky. In either case you'll want to swim along the shoreline on the right. The area out to the immediate left offers nothing but murky water. Runoff from a storm several years back dumped a lot of sediment that killed off the coral.

Swimming along the right side will soon put you into fish as the shoreline rocks form a ledge descending into deep water. Follow it along, exploring as you go. It will bend further to the right and you'll see lots of little areas to check out. When you reach the first point jutting out into the water, round it and you'll find an area offering a multitude of possibilities. You can

Stareye Parrotfish and Saddle Wrasse

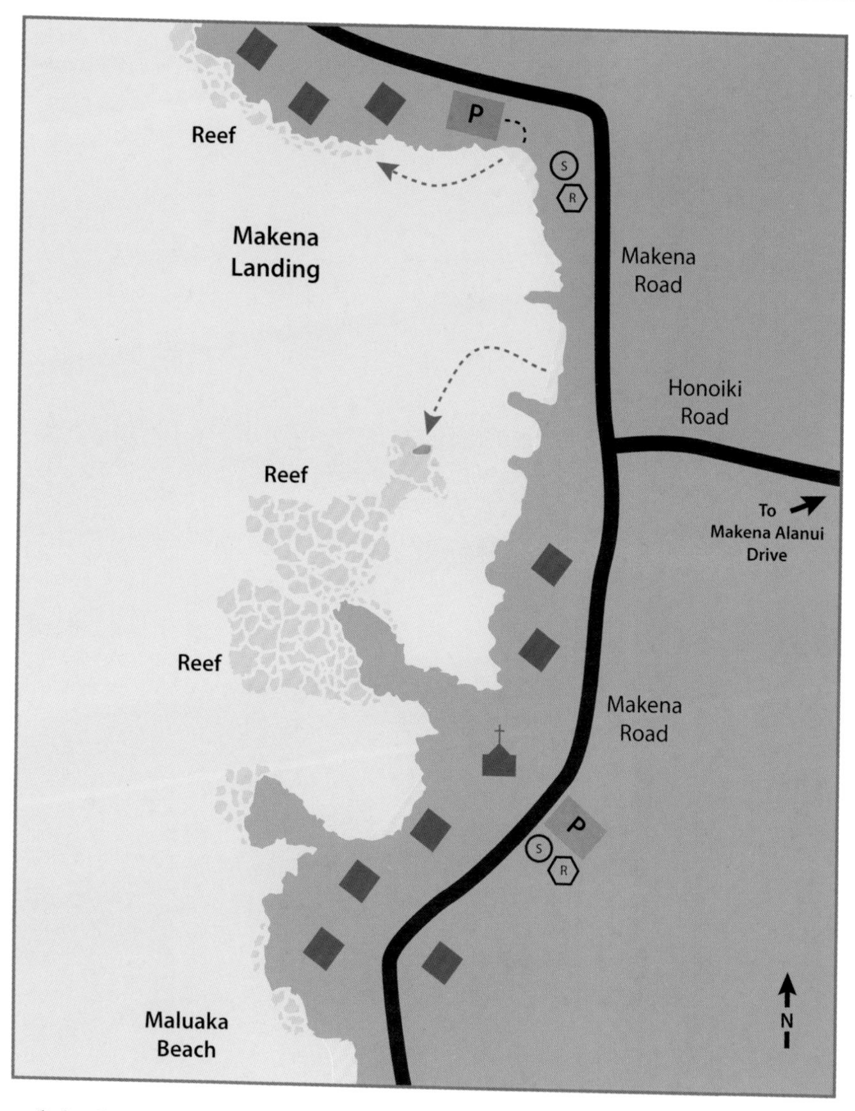

glide above the canyons below, snorkel over to the next point, or follow the reef further out from shore.

Proceeding along the reef will take you into deeper water as you move farther from shore. Depths will vary, rising and falling along the way. There's a shelf about 125 yards out from the first point that hosts a ton of fish and some very pretty coral. It's an amazing place when you have it to yourself. Just off this shelf snorkel tours often drop anchor.

Bluefin Trevallies

If it gets crowded, move on in the general direction of the second point. Much like the first, it offers great snorkeling and an underwater ledge to explore.

Depending how much meandering you've done, you're getting close to the half-mile mark. Reversing course and heading back will have provided enough for most snorkelers, but if you're up for it, there's still plenty to see.

Heading inland on this shelf and past the second point offers some beautiful coral. As the depths gives way to shallower water look for eels. They like to hide in the crevices of coral and rocks. Making your way along the shoreline leads to a narrow, channel-like cove. This is the Five Caves - Five Graves entry. Along the rocks and pockets just north of this entrance is the location of some underwater caves. They're said to be resting spots for Whitetip Reef Sharks, but it's doubtful you'll see them. Unlike most sharks, whitetips can rest in place and don't need to swim to keep water moving through their gills. While not known for aggressive behavior, please don't harass them. I once witnessed a snorkeler grab a six-footer by the tail. Lucky for him he wasn't bitten, but the shark swam away and the chance for others to see it was lost.

Past the rocky ledges north of Five Caves - Five Graves you'll find areas of coral 20-30 yards out. You can make your way through here ignoring the first cove. The second cove and the points that mark it are all interesting to snorkel. The water is quite variable in clarity and it gets a little shallow in the cove, but you'll often find a wide variety of fish. Be sure to scan the water near the surface. Needlefish tend to hang right near the top and are a frequent sight along this cove. If you round the reef on the north side, you'll arrive at Chang's Beach. It's a perfect place to take a breather on the sand. If you've meandered all the way from Makena Landing, you've snorkeled nearly a mile. Impressive.

Yellowmargin Moray

Before heading back, be sure to check out the reef on the north side of Chang's Beach. It can sometimes be cloudy, but when the water is clear it's unbeatable for its beauty.

A marathon snorkel awaits around the point.

A juvenile sea turtle rests among the coral.

Snorkeling directly back you'll cover just over a half-mile. As an option, if you bring reef shoes in a mesh bag you can walk along the road from Chang's Beach, but it's a half-mile with a hill. You can also exit at Five Caves - Five Graves and cut the walk down to a quarter-mile.

If you're interested in snorkeling the southern section of Makena Landing, your best bet is to hike down the road to the last beach before Makena Road intersects Honoiki. It's roughly 300 yards from the parking lot. Enter the water and swim south to the jumble of rocks breaking the water's surface about 80 yards from shore. There's not much to see along the way—nothing really—but when you round the west side of the rocks you'll enter the start of a gorgeous area. If the water is clear, and that's the gamble with this spot, the snorkeling is awesome. Beautiful large coral heads extend into the distance and you'll see plenty of turtles, morays, and large fish.

Take note, it's a fairly long swim and water clarity is never a sure thing, factors that will undoubtedly keep it off most people's list. But for the adventure snorkeler, I highly recommend it. It's definitely one of my favorite spots.

Pacific Trumpetfish and Convict Tangs

Location: South Maui, Makena Road, about 2½ miles south of Wailea.

From Wailea, drive 2½ miles south on Wailea Alanui Road / Makena Alanui Road and turn right on Honoiki Road. Proceed to Makena Road and turn right. You'll see Makena Landing Beach Park on your left.

Maluaka Beach

Maluaka is a true gem and one of my favorite beaches in South Maui. It's a peaceful spot in a beautiful setting and offers fantastic snorkeling. Blessed with a wide stretch of sand it provides offshore views from Molokini to the West Maui Mountains. Bordered by the picturesque grounds of the Makena Beach and Golf Resort, Maluaka has showers and bathrooms, decent parking, and is relatively uncrowded compared to other Maui beaches. It's the perfect place for a morning snorkel followed by a day of picnicking, swimming, and enjoying the beach.

Maluaka is framed with rock points that offer interesting sights in either direction, but the best snorkeling is found at the south end of the beach. The expansive reef is home to one of Maui's famed "Turtle Towns," where excursion boats often bring paying customers—it's that good. There's also an abundance of great coral, a wide variety of fish, and dramatic underwater seascapes with ravines, arches, and hidden caverns. It's a fantastic place to explore, made even better by the fact that you can enjoy it for free.

The reef on the south starts where the sand meets the rocks and hugs the lava shoreline as it extends out to sea. At the point, it turns back toward the north and is a great place to find eels, large box fish, and the occasional octopus. Closer to shore and back near the point, the

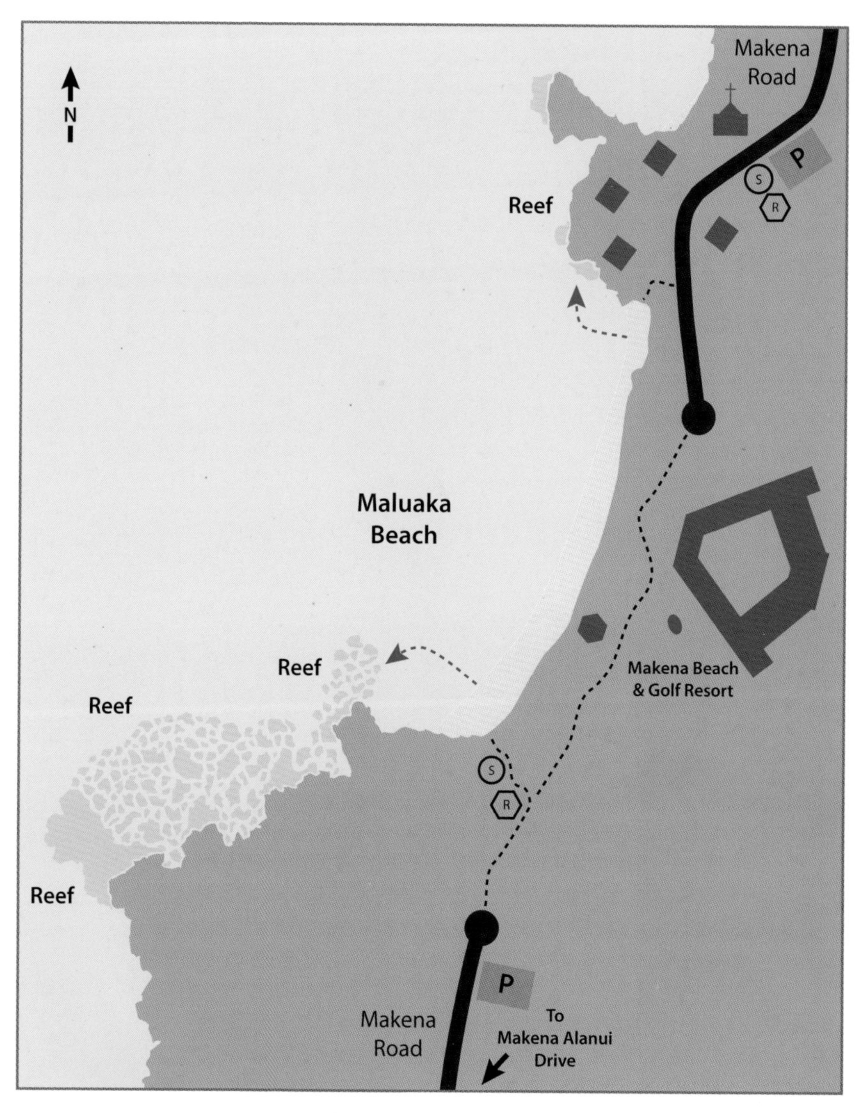

reef narrows through the first cove, then widens back out, extending in an arch out and around for over two hundred yards. It's an expansive area offering endless exploration with abundant marine life. Turtles are common, as are eels, trumpetfish, porcupinefish, and triggerfish. On one outing, I even encountered a reef shark and a Magnificent Snake Eel—pretty cool. It's not often you'll see either one of them, let alone both on the same day.

Maluaka's north end offers snorkeling potential, but it's much less

Spotted Eagle Ray

extensive until you reach a triangle-shaped peninsula. Even then, the water is fairly shallow and can sometimes be cloudy. The reef starts a few yards from the beach, then closely mirrors the shoreline around to the peninsula. While I've never encountered huge numbers of fish, I once saw a juvenile Spotted Eagle Ray cruising the edge of the beach.

Facilities: Restrooms and showers. The beautifully manicured resort grounds and undeveloped greens along the southern shoreline offer nice areas to walk and explore.

Snorkeling: To snorkel the south end, enter the water about 15 yards before reaching the rocks. The water near shore can often be cloudy, so it's best to swim out twenty yards or so before angling toward the reef. Begin scanning the ocean floor as soon as you don your mask. Several small coral heads can be found scattered close to shore and you may come across a Picasso Triggerfish before reaching the reef. Preferring sandy areas, they're remarkably beautiful, but extremely shy. At least that's been my experience after several unsuccessful attempts to get a picture. Most people miss them, so take your time. Sporting a blue band above their eyes, yellow lips, and "painted" sides, their colors are amazing and seeing one is a real treat.

When you reach the reef, follow its edge as it continues north then enter when something captures your attention. Water depths will vary

Magnificent Snake Eel

considerably. Take plenty of time to explore the pockets and carefully scan the coral. I've found more than a few octopuses through here, but they're extremely easy to miss. One day I was entertained by two interacting on the same small coral head while other snorkelers swam by, completely missing the show.

When you're ready to move on, follow the reef south back toward the point. Bypass the first cove as its sandy bottom tends to cloud the water. A short swim across will get you back into awesome snorkeling. From here, you have a huge expanse to roam. The reef spreads out from shore for over 100 yards and extends another 200 yards south. Entering the inner reef, you'll find massive coral heads interspersed with intriguing channels. Turtles are regulars here—I've never failed to see one. At the outer south edge of the reef a steep drop from the coral plateau offers a vertical wall pocked with overhanging ledges. It's also the site of my first reef shark encounter. I was all alone, the water was slightly cloudy, and that first glimpse gave me quite a start—"WOW" is right!

See the octopus?

Experienced snorkelers can make their way around the point and arrive on the north end of

Black Sand Beach. A 175 yard swim will get you to the sand. As you reach the shoreline, the water can be cloudy so look out for hidden rocks. If you plan to walk back, be sure to bring reef shoes. I put mine in a mesh bag tied at my waist. Whether I need them or not, it keeps my options open.

To snorkel the north end of Maluaka, enter the water about twenty yards before the rocks. Take care. Shifting sand occasionally exposes toe-busting rocks close to shore and the pain they deliver can be surprising. Once you're in the water swim out about 20 yards and head toward the rocky shoreline. Follow it as far as you desire. If conditions are good and you're up for a marathon trip, you can snorkel all they up to the kayak launch site at Makena Landing. Fantastic snorkeling can be found near an offshore rock just south of Makena Landing. Read more about it in the Makena Landing section (p. 142).

Location: South Maui, Makena Road, just beyond Makena Golf & Beach Resort.

From Wailea, drive south on Wailea Alanui Road / Makena Alanui Road to Makena Golf and Beach Resort. Just past the resort, turn right on Makena Road. It's a dead end spur of the same Makena Road found

Humuhumunukunukuapua'a - Hawaii's State Fish

Juvenile Green Sea Turtle

on the north side of the resort. There are a few parking spots at the turn around, but a larger area can be found just before it on your right. Follow the resort's walkway from the parking area through the grounds and take the first branch to the beach by the restrooms and showers.

Additional parking can be found on the north side of the resort on Makena Road. Backtrack on Makena Alanui Road to just north of the Makena Beach and Golf Resort. Turn west on Honoiki Street. Make a left on Makena Road and you'll see a public parking area across from a small chapel. This lot also has showers and restrooms, and short walk down the road will bring you to the north end of the beach. If you have a group or a lot of gear, there's also a nice pull off at the beach to unload before parking.

Pu'u Ola'i from Black Sand Beach

Little Beach

Compared to Big Beach next door, Little Beach is just as it sounds. Tucked away at the base of Pu'u Ola'i (Red Hill), it's reached by a short hike up Big Beach. This secluded spot offers an easy sandy entry and nice snorkeling off both its points. When conditions are calm, it's also the gateway to an adventure-snorkel all the way around to Black Sand Beach to the north. While not teeming with fish, the area offers decent numbers and interesting rock formations with coves, crevices, and a variety of coral to explore along the way.

If you're uncomfortable with nudity, you may want to skip the visit. Little Beach is popular with the "clothing optional" crowd. That doesn't mean you have to shed your clothes, but it's very likely you'll see others who have shed theirs. So be prepared, it's quite a sight when you're snorkeling back to the beach and see an adult male swimming along in his birthday suit! Personally, I'd be afraid a curious fish might just take a bite. Yet another reason not to feed the fish.

Facilities: Portable restrooms at the Big Beach parking area.

Snorkeling: Entry is made on the right side of the beach about 25 yards before the shoreline rocks. Initially the water may be cloudy, but

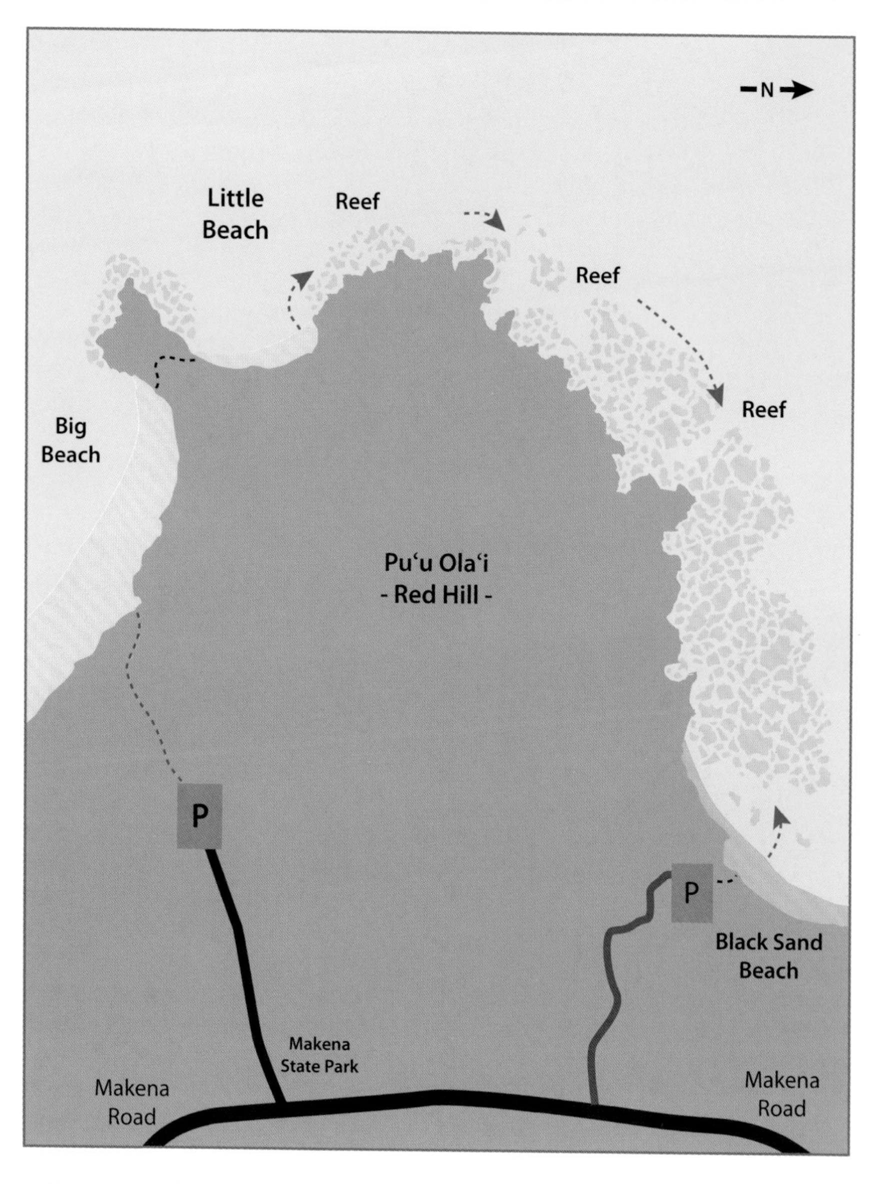

clarity usually improves as you move away from the beach. Making your way along the shoreline provides plenty of to see with interesting topography and marine life. We were swimming through here, when out of the deep a Spotted Eagle Ray cruised directly toward us. It disappeared as quickly as it appeared, but what an amazing moment. While eagle rays aren't nearly as large as their manta cousins, this guy was huge. Their polka-dotted back-sides make them uniquely beautiful creatures to see.

If you're up for the adventure to Black Sand Beach, continue along to the right. As you round the shoreline you'll see a distinct rocky point. If the current is running toward you, it can make for a challenging swim to get around the point, but a nice cruise on the way back. If the current is running with you (in the direction of your snorkel path) it can make for a tough trip back. Gauge its force by reversing direction and swimming against it. If you can't move through it with ease, forget rounding the point. A return swim would be exhausting and the lava cliffs don't provide much of a land option.

If conditions are good, give the little cove just before the point a wide berth. The current collects much of the debris that floats through here and holds it in a swirling eddy. Nicknamed the "toilet bowl" by those in the know, it isn't much fun to swim through.

Needlefish swim just below the surface

Around the point the shoreline provides several interesting coves to snorkel. I once found one packed with a school of needlefish skimming the surface. Swimming out from shore puts you in deeper water quickly. The area offers an interesting mix of coral and boulder fields to explore, along with a good chance of seeing turtles and eels.

Continue along as your comfort and desire allows, but don't forget it's a long swim back to Little Beach. As the day progresses, the winds and waves pick up. If you make it all the way to Black Sand Beach, you may want to relax on shore before your return. Watch for rocks and coral heads close to the shoreline and pick your exit and entry route carefully.

Whitemouth Moray Eel

Location: South Maui, Makena Alanui Road, 4 miles south of Wailea.

From Wailea, drive south on Wailea Alanui Road / Makena Alanui Road for about 4 miles. As you pass Pu'u Ola'i(the big red hill), you'll see the paved entrance to Makena State Park on your right. Look for a shady spot and grab your gear. It's a good idea not to leave valuables behind.

Take the trail to the beach. Follow the beach to the right until it ends at the base of the hill. A short trail cut into the ledge will take you to the other side. It's an easy scramble and once you're up and over, you're there.

Ahihi Cove

Most guidebooks and magazines give Ahihi Cove great reviews. You'll also see lots of people snorkeling here. To be honest, I don't get it. I've always found this spot to have horrible visibility and not worth the time. It's possible I've never hit it on a good day, but I've certainly found far superior places to snorkel and one of them is just up the road at Ahihi Bay—also called "The Dumps."

On the plus side, Ahihi Cove is usually quite calm, very pretty, and located about as close to the road as you can get. Shelves of lava rock surround the water and Kiawe trees provide a little shade. Bright yellow tangs often frequent the cove and shallows along Makena Road. If you decide to give Ahihi a try, hopefully you'll find clear water and a few tangs paying a visit. Parking can be tight, with a couple of spots across the road and a few more on the ocean side just past the cove. If needed, you can always park at the Ahihi Bay lot and walk back.

Facilities: None. Portable restrooms at the Ahihi Bay parking lot.

Snorkeling: Access the cove from the right side where the remnants of an old boat launch provide a gradual entry. Watch for urchins and take it slow, it can be slick. After exploring the inner cove, the larger

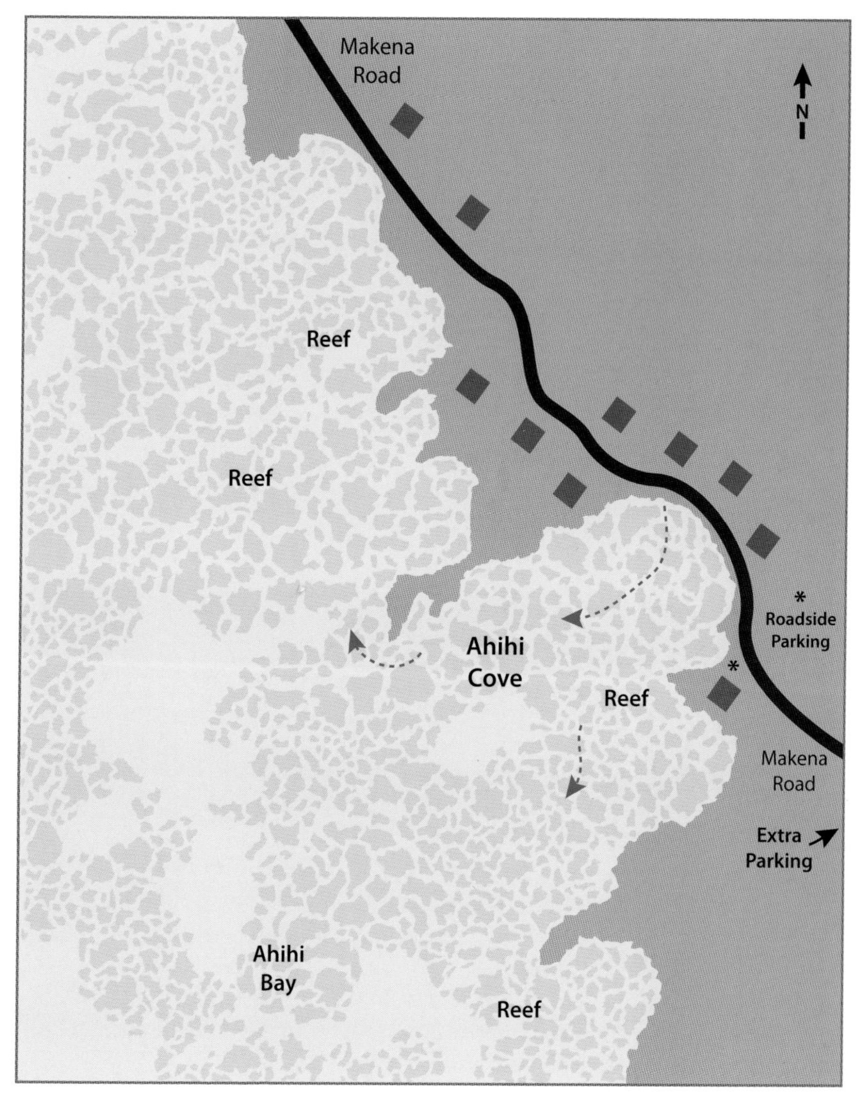

portion of Ahihi Bay offers interesting snorkeling. If the water is not rough, swimming to the right provides several lava outcroppings with good-sized fish. The gravel area just north of Ahihi Cove is a good spot to turn back.

Snorkeling the left side of the cove takes you toward Ahihi Bay. You'll find better snorkeling the further you go. Water clarity can vary, but you'll likely see plenty of fish and a turtle or two. Good swimmers can continue to the Ahihi Bay / Dumps snorkel area, easily identified by the

Yellow Tang

number of visitors and gear scattered along the shoreline rocks. It's a great area with plenty to see, but at nearly a half-mile from the cove it's better accessed from down the road.

Location: South Maui, Makena Alanui Road, 5 miles south of Wailea.

From Wailea, drive south on Wailea Alanui Road/ Makena Alanui Road. After 4½ miles, the road will begin to hug the shoreline and you'll see signs marking the entrance to the Ahihi-Kina'u Natural Area Reserve. At just over 5 miles, you'll arrive at Ahihi Cove. If there's no parking, more can be found a quarter-mile down the road at a large parking area for Ahihi Bay. Look for it on your right, you'll see a yellow gate marking the entrance to a lava rock parking lot with portable restrooms.

Green Sea Turtle looking for a spot to rest

Ahihi Bay

Despite its nickname, “The Dumps” is one of the top snorkel spots in South Maui. It covers a vast area, has a lot of fish with good size and variety, and it’s rare not to encounter a turtle here. There’s a ton to see and it’s easy to spend a couple hours snorkeling the coral heads or journeying to Ahihi Cove and beyond.

Water clarity at Ahihi Bay can be a mixed bag. It can vary considerably from one day to the next, throughout the area, and as the day progresses. As a general rule conditions are better in the morning. When the winds pick up, the water gets rougher and visibility begins to suffer. While the area rarely feels crowded, arriving early is your best bet for smaller crowds and better conditions.

Ahihi Bay is located along the rocky shores of a lava field within the Ahihi-Kinaʻu Reserve. The snorkeling here is usually quite good and benefits from the ban on fishing and a minimal amount of sand. Unfortunately if you’re not in the water enjoying the sights, there’s little to do and its rocky shores severely lack comfort.

It’s definitely not a great spot for kids. It’s better to come here with experienced snorkelers, hit the water early, then head to Maluaka Beach to rinse off and relax.

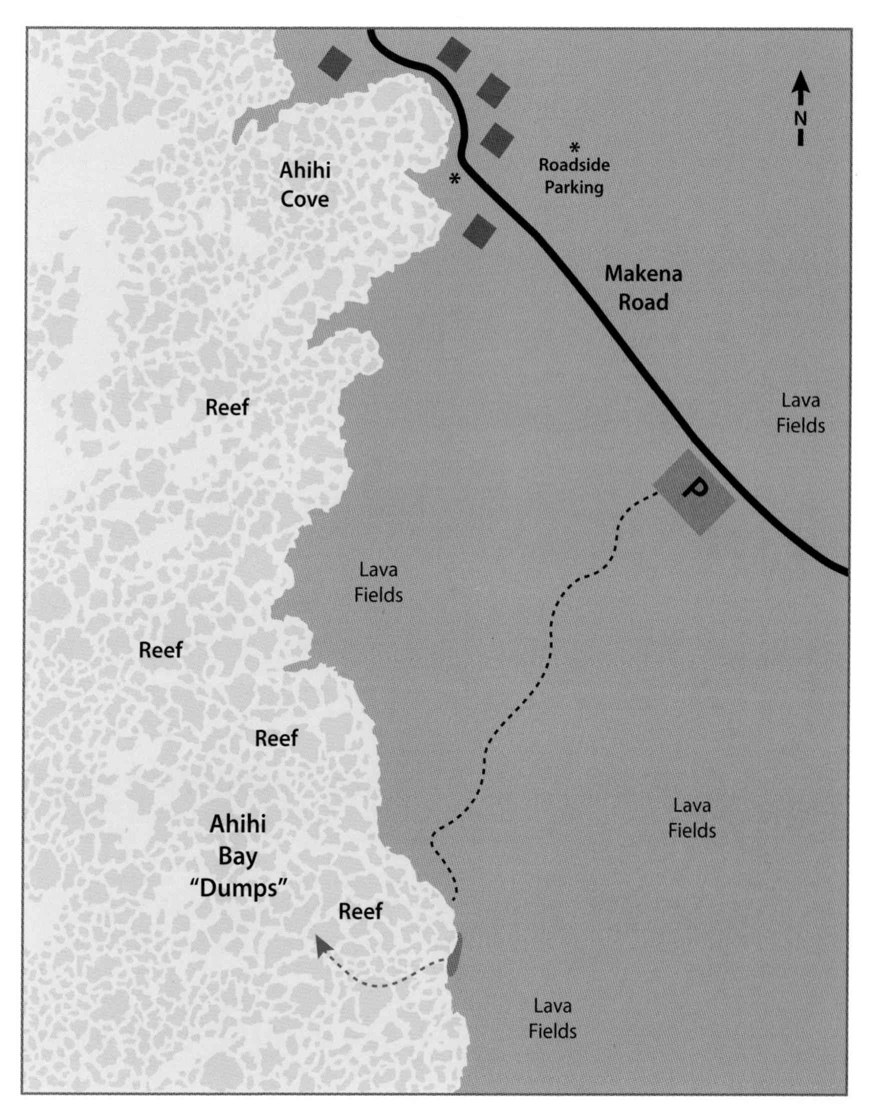

Facilities: Portable restrooms at the parking area.

Snorkeling: The best spot to enter the water is at the far end of the beach, just before the lava rock outcropping. It has fewer obstructions once you're in the water, but take care on the slippery rock shelf as you enter. It's easy to take a spill. The water at the entry can often be cloudy, but it clears as you proceed from shore. Snorkel straight out and skip

Bluefin Trevally

the initial coral head to your right, you can check it out on your way back and there's much better stuff ahead. Twenty-five yards straight out should put you in about twenty feet of water and over some very pretty coral. Get your bearings here and start exploring.

If you swim to the left, you'll find pockets of beautiful coral and a nice range of larger fish, but the clarity is often poor. Swimming to the right is much better. If you meander toward shore and back out again, slowly making your way to the right, you'll cover some very nice territory. The area is a maze of crevices between lava rocks and coral heads with depths ranging from 25 feet to just inches. Take your time gliding through here and you're sure to see some amazing fish. Large surgeonfish, unicornfish, and parrotfish are all common. I've also encountered a massive Bluefin Trevally at the same spot on several visits. These intimidating looking fish are impressive to watch as they patrol their territory.

As you continue making your way to the right you'll encounter patches of sand extending to shore. If the water is rough, these areas can be cloudy. Swimming further along will bring you back into clearer water until the next patch. Along the way, you'll be hard pressed not to come upon a few turtles. I've snorkeled and dove here many times and can't remember not seeing one. Called Honu by Hawaiians, sea turtles have a life span of 80 years or more. Please enjoy them at a distance, it's

Paletail Unicornfish

healthier for the turtles and can save you some big bucks. Harassing them can bring huge fines.

Experienced snorkelers can make their way over to Ahihi Cove and beyond. It's a great excursion, but a half-mile swim. If you're thinking about it, consider towing your reef shoes in a net bag. It keeps your options open if you decide to hike back. We learned the hard way while making this walk in bare feet. It's not bad along the road, but the lava rock parking area is torture. It gets even worse hiking the lava trail to your bags, towels, and car keys left at the shoreline. No wonder it's called A'a' rock! It's hard to imagine ancient Hawaiians ran across this stuff regularly.

If you snorkel into Ahihi Cove, you'll likely find it cloudy. Other than providing an entry point to the larger bay, I don't understand the attraction here for snorkelers. Regardless, it's always busy when we drive by. If you exit here, veer to the left. At the shoreline you'll find the remnants of an old boat ramp. Watch your footing, it can be slick and harbor urchins.

If the surf isn't rolling you can snorkel among the lava outcroppings found just past Ahihi Cove. The fish here can be big. I've come across trumpet and cornetfish that appeared to surpass their official size range. I've also encountered a school of Bluefin Trevallies just offshore from the gravel area north of the cove. This area marks the edge of the marine preserve and is a good spot to turn around. If you've made it this far, you're officially a snorkel fanatic. Welcome to the club!

Orangeband Surgeonfish

Oval Butterflyfish

Location: South Maui, Makena Alanui Road, 5½ miles south of Wailea.

From Wailea, drive south on Wailea Alanui Road/ Makena Alanui Road. After 4½ miles the road will hug the shoreline and provide a chance to check the conditions and decide what type of snorkel outing seems reasonable. You'll soon enter the Ahihi-Kinaʻu Natural Area Reserve. At just over 5 miles, you'll come to a small protected cove—Ahihi Cove. A quarter-mile further, you'll see a yellow gate on your right for the Ahihi Bay parking area. Find a spot and follow the short trail through the lava field. When you reach the rocky shoreline, head to the far end so you'll be closer to the entry.

Blue Spine Unicornfish – In Watercolor

La Pérouse Bay

La Pérouse Bay is usually rough, murky, and extremely windy. On very rare occasions it may be different, but it's worse than hit and miss—more like miss, miss, and miss. Why waste your valuable vacation time on a bad snorkel outing? This is Maui. Great snorkel spots are all over the place. My advice is to pick another spot. It's an interesting place to visit, just leave your snorkeling gear behind.

The bay is located at the end of Makena Alanui Road in the midst of an old lava flow. It's a rugged area with a parking lot that will take its toll on your vehicle if you're not careful. When the pavement ends, drive slowly and pick your course wisely. There is plenty of parking near the shoreline.

La Pérouse is often listed as a snorkeling destination and at one time the snorkeling here was termed "good." But that was really a description of the coves out and around the lava shoreline to the right. Those areas are now off-limits and word has it they're unlikely to re-open. If they do, keep in mind it's a healthy swim and conditions here can get rough quickly. Early morning is always your best bet.

Facilities: Portable Restrooms.

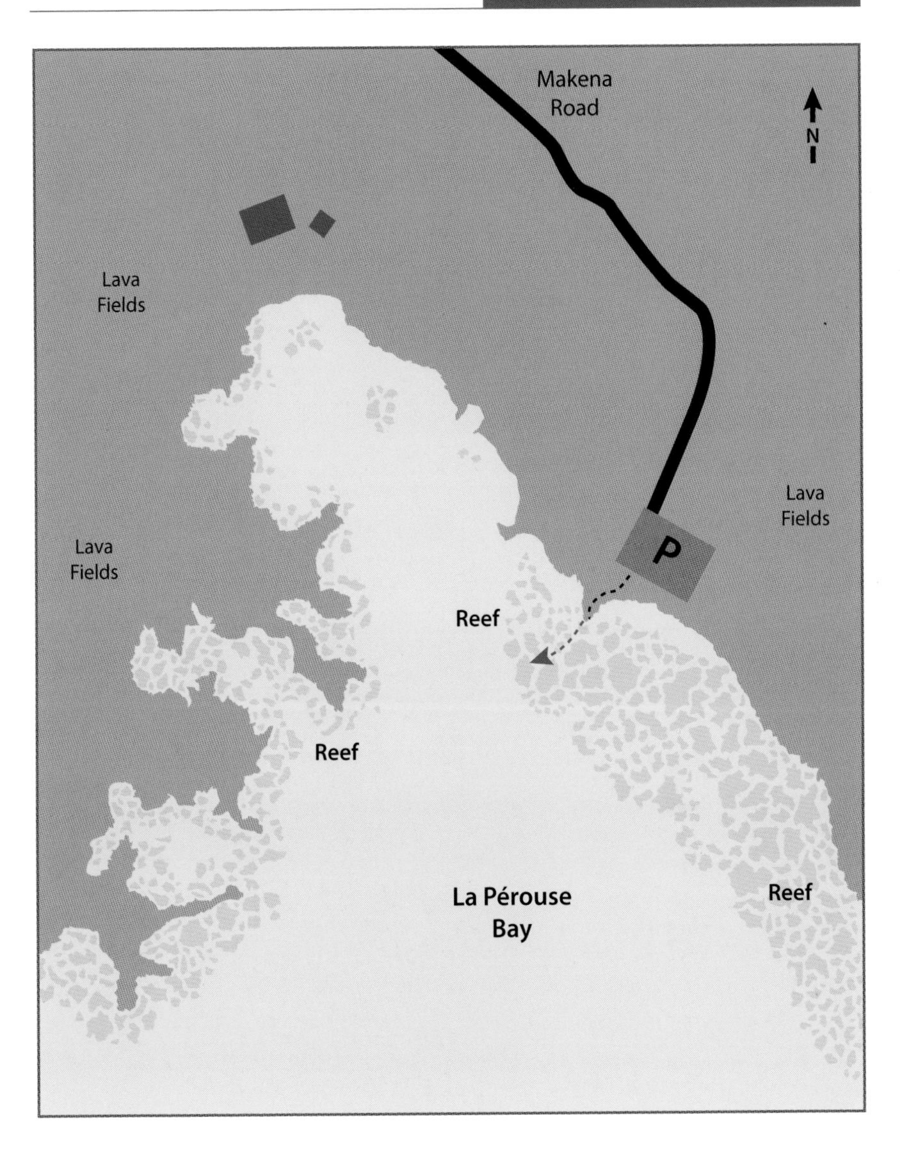

Snorkeling: Entry is a few yards left of the rock wall / fence line. You'll see a lava shelf that extends into the water. At its far end is a ledge with a drop-off into about three feet of water. This is a good place to gear up and enter. Watch for surge. It's easy to get banged-up here even when things don't look particularly crazy. As you explore, always keep track of the conditions and the arrival of the daily winds.

Evening at La Pérouse Bay

Location: South Maui, Makena Alanui Road, 7 miles south of Wailea.

From Wailea, drive south on Wailea Alanui Road / Wailea Makena Road. At about 5 miles you'll begin driving through a massive lava field.

From here-on the road becomes one lane with pullouts to accommodate oncoming traffic. When the pavement ends, you've reached La Pérouse. A few parking spots can be found to your immediate left, or continue 150 yards around the corner and you'll arrive at the water's edge.

Kayak Excursions

If you're up for an adventure and can handle a little exercise, a great way to snorkel some of Maui's best spots is from a kayak. It's a blast and an experience you're unlikely to forget. Whether you go on your own or with a local kayaking outfit, you're able cover a lot of ground and hit the water before most people are even on the beach. If kayaking the waters of Maui sounds like something you'd like to try, you have two options:

Guided Kayak Snorkel Tours: These outfitters provide everything you need, often throw in lunch, and do a good job leading their tours to some of the best spots. They charge around $70 a person for a half-day outing and operate frequently out of Makena Landing in South Maui and Olowalu in West Maui. Some also offer trips along the "Pali Cliffs" tunnel area and from DT Fleming to Honolua Bay. While I've never been a paying customer on Maui, I've encountered them often and have been impressed with many of their guides. Most are knowledgeable, friendly, and intent on providing you with a great experience. They also don't overload their tours, so when you reach a snorkel spot you're not facing a crowd. It's a great option and if you're looking for local knowledge and added direction, give them a call. You will thoroughly enjoy the experience.

Unguided Excursions: If you're confident in your abilities and like to go your own way, skip the tours and rent a kayak. Several beachfront hotels make it easy by renting kayaks right at the beach. But be warned, the price for the convenience is usually steep. A more cost effective option may be to contact a few of the kayak tour operators to find out who is renting and where you can pick it up. Locations can vary, but with advanced reservations, morning excursions out of Makena Landing seem to be a fairly consistent offering. Some operators also allow you to pick up a kayak from their yards and provide roof racks and straps. There's also the option of renting from individual owners. Craigslist Maui frequently has ads offering multiple-day rentals at really good prices. Transport and nightly storage might present a hurdle, but if you can overcome it, this may be your all-around best bet. Renting a kayak for a couple of days provides the freedom to explore multiple spots on your own schedule.

Moloka'i in the distance - West Maui

Tips for Unguided Excursions

Wind: When you're kayaking in Maui, it's important to remember that the wind will pick up as the day progresses. Along West Maui, this means an offshore wind pushing you further out to sea. It can be a tough fight paddling against it and if it gets really crazy, you may not make it back. So take heed, if the wind starts, head closer to shore or come in completely. Reports of kayakers requiring rescue are a common sight in the local paper. In South Maui, the wind usually blows along the shoreline, rather than out to sea. While not as punishing as offshore winds, they can still present a strenuous challenge returning to your launch site. A good rule of thumb is to plan for wind as you're paddling back. Regardless of what the conditions were at the start of the day, it always seems you're fighting wind on your return. So know your limits and save some energy for the full length of your trip.

Anchor: Once you reach a snorkel spot, you'll need to ensure the kayak doesn't drift away while you're out snorkeling. The easiest way is to drop an anchor. I have a small one that I take along on every excursion. It's not particularly heavy, but for a kayak it does a great job.

Anchored in a cove north of Namalu Bay

Ask about getting one if you're renting, it's a nice option. When you're ready to drop anchor, make sure it's deployed in a patch of sand and not smashing around on the coral. If you can't get your hands on an anchor, don't worry. With a little nylon rope you can tether the kayak to your wrist and pull it along behind you or have a partner remain in the kayak and shadow your path. On marathon excursions I usually do all three. The important thing is keeping the kayak from drifting away. A lost kayak, especially on Maui, can be a spendy proposition!

Additional Gear: Be sure to bring drinking water, sunglasses, and sunscreen. Wearing a hat, T-shirt, or a skin can also provide great

protection from extended time in the sun. If you want to be extra cautious, a cell phone in a dry bag isn't a bad idea. Just know that a kayak is not a dry place so plan on everything getting wet. Finally, have a plan for your car keys. A carabiner works great to attach your keys to yourself or your kayak, you definitely don't want them "lost at sea!"

Olowalu

Olowalu has some of the oldest and most unique coral on Maui. On a nice day with clear water it's incredible. You'll find the best snorkeling about 600 yards offshore—look for the kayak tours. They paddle out around 8 am, tie off together, and drop anchor. You can't miss them. The near shore waters are very shallow and you'll need to carefully snake your way around numerous coral heads that dot the area. It's tricky navigating with some spots mere inches below the surface so take care to avoid them with your kayak and paddles.

When you near the snorkel area, start looking for patches of sand to position your anchor. They're plentiful so don't feel the need to closely shadow the kayak tours. The coral out here is immense and beautiful, rising from depths of 30 feet to just below the surface and interspersed with underwater pathways and canyons. Turtle sightings and large numbers of fish are common. But be warned, as the sign back on shore states, "Sharks May be Present." I've never seen a shark here and statistically the likelihood is extremely low, but there have been attacks in the area as well as a fatality. This knowledge is the one thing that keeps me from enjoying Olowalu to its fullest. I'll admit the "Jaws" theme song is my frequent companion while snorkeling these waters. Even so, it's one of my favorite spots.

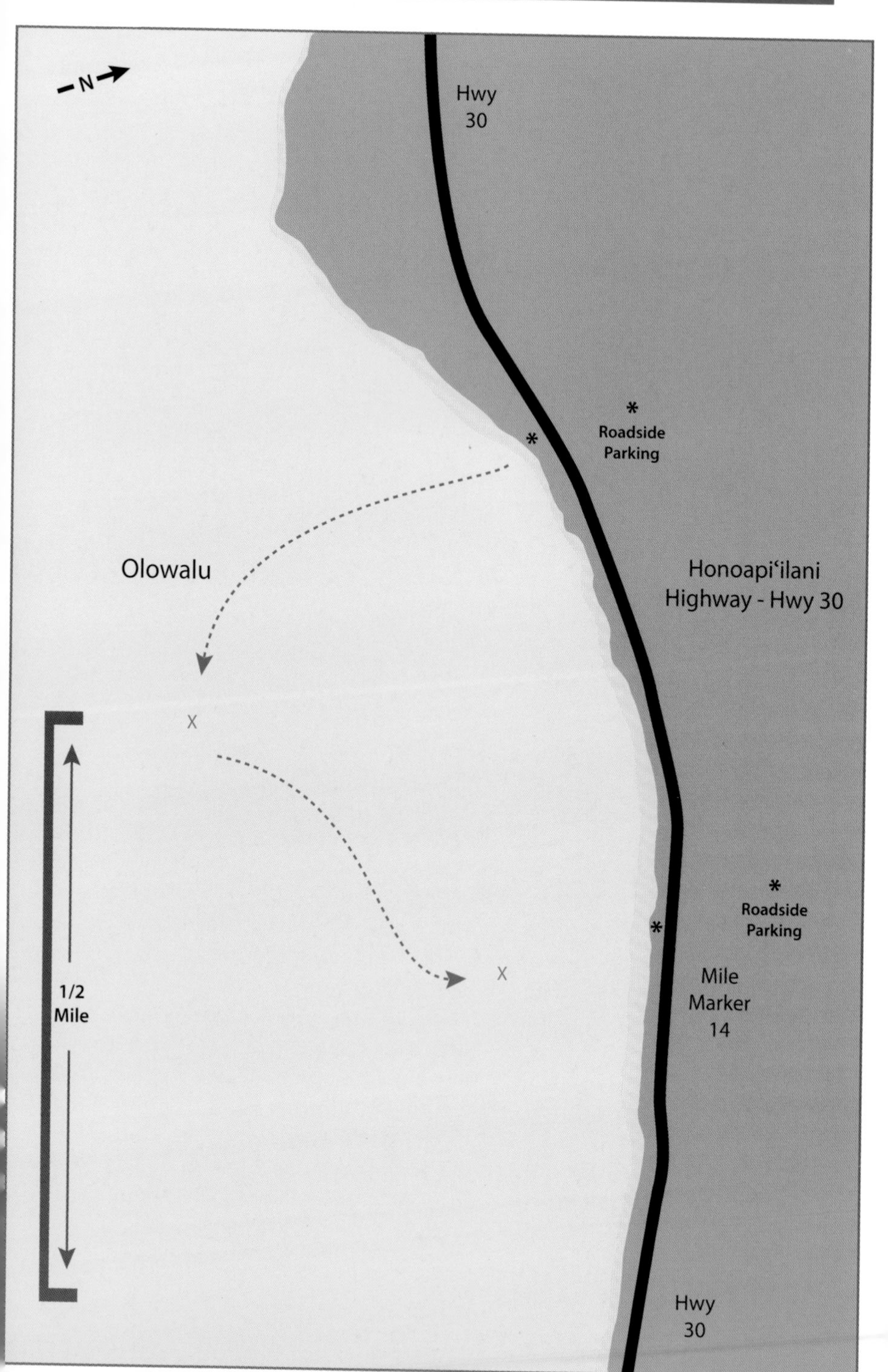
N
Hwy
30
Roadside
Parking
Olowalu
Honoapi'ilani
Highway - Hwy 30
X
1/2
Mile
Roadside
Parking
X
Mile
Marker
14
Hwy
30

Kayak snorkeling off Olowalu

Water clarity can vary widely within a few yards. If you find it less than ideal, you can swim to another spot without resetting your anchor. Once you're ready to see more of Olowalu, paddle toward shore in a southerly direction and angle your way toward the snorkel spot at mile marker 14. If you're unsure of the location, look for snorkelers along the shoreline to get a heading—there are usually plenty of them. Avoid going completely to shore as it becomes extremely shallow. Instead, find a place around 100 yards out where you can drop anchor, slip into the water and explore. Clarity can be an issue here, but if it's nice there are beautiful stretches of coral and lots of meandering channels to keep you busy. When you've had your fill, return to the launch site. It's an easy half-mile.

Distance: 1½ miles round trip.

Facilities: Portable restrooms along the roadside beach areas.

Location: West Maui, Highway 30, half-mile north of mile marker 14.

From Lahaina, drive south on Hwy 30 for roughly 5½ miles. Just south of Camp Olowalu, look for a sandy pull out and parking area on the ocean side of the road. You'll know you're close once you've passed the Olowalu Store and the last of the cool Monkeypod trees along the road. If you're coming from the south, the pull-off is four miles north of the tunnel—a half-mile past MM 14.

The Pali "Cliffs"

This excursion is definitely an adventurous trek and not for everyone. Make sure to get an early start in the morning, and if you're uncertain of your abilities skip it or call it good at the tunnel. If you continue to the Scenic Lookout, understand the route crosses several gaps in the West Maui Mountains and the wind tunneling through them can create trouble. Either way, you'll find the best snorkeling in the first half of the excursion—the rest is pure adventure.

Launching here is easy. You can park close to the shore and avoid lugging your kayak far. Once in the water, be careful of the breakers and the shallow reef just a few yards off shore. Navigate past it and head south to an area right off the point. This spot is known as the Coral Gardens. It's a good place to anchor and the surrounding hundred yards provides an intriguing area to explore. Let water clarity be your guide and enjoy. A carpet of coral offers treasures in all directions.

When you're ready to move on, follow the shoreline into the first cove. If you haven't snorkeled yet, it's difficult to stay out of the water. Towing your kayak through here is a nice option. The second cove is less impressive but still worth checking out. A jumble of boulders rim the shore and numerous fish hide among them.

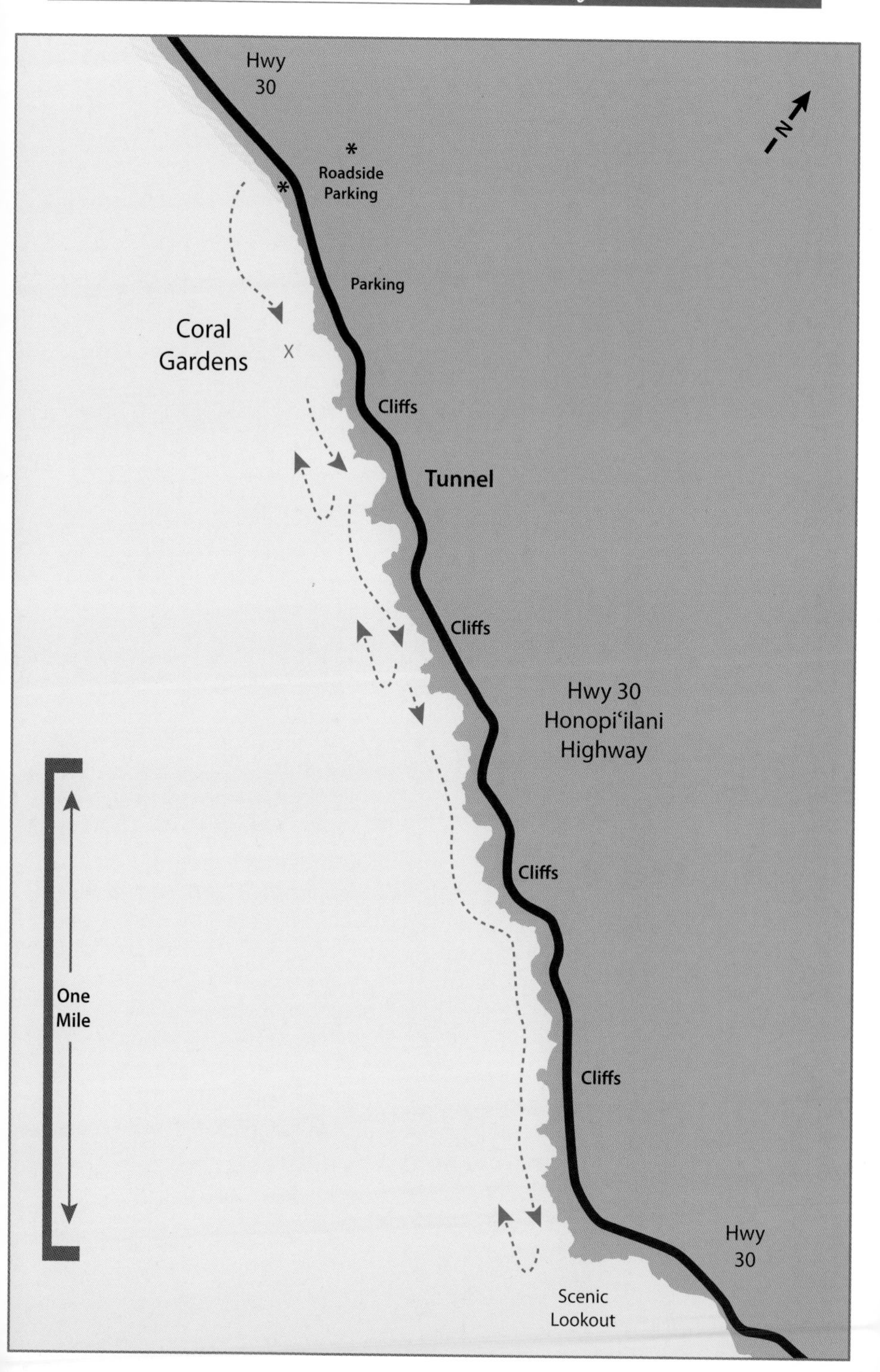
Hwy
30
N
*
Roadside
Parking
*
Parking
Coral
Gardens
X
Cliffs
Tunnel
Cliffs
Hwy 30
Honopiʻilani
Highway
Cliffs
One
Mile
Cliffs
Hwy
30
Scenic
Lookout

A kayak tour off the "pali"—the Hawaiian word for cliffs

The next two coves are below each side of the tunnel and are also interesting to explore. Don't be surprised to find a kayak snorkel tour anchored in one of them. If you've had enough, the return trip should be an easy paddle; it's just under three-quarters of a mile.

If you're feeling adventurous, reaching the area below the scenic lookout requires another mile and a half of paddling. Make sure to hug the cliffs for the windbreak and watch for swells, particularly off the points. There are a few spots with shallow underwater ledges that can kick up some serious danger if you're not paying attention. Remember you're "on your own" out here. While situated just below a major highway, the steep cliffs make your location very remote and challenging to access if you get into trouble. Continuing along the cliffs offers several more coves for your enjoyment and reaching the waters under the lookout provides a sense of accomplishment. If you complete the full excursion count yourself in a small group of adventurers who have made this trip while visiting Maui.

I've heard the snorkeling below the lookout is great. Unfortunately, I can't provide an opinion as time and conditions kept me from enjoying

it. The waters looked pretty amazing though—I guess there's always next time. If the conditions are right and you have time for a snorkel, don't forget about the wind. It picks up as the day progresses and the return trip is over two miles of serious paddling.

Distance: 1½ miles round trip to the tunnel; or 4¾ miles round trip to the Scenic Lookout.

Facilities: Portable restrooms at Papalaua Wayside.

Location: West Maui, Highway 30, just south of mile marker 11.

From Lahaina, drive south on Hwy 30 for about 9 miles. Parking can be found at the south end of Papalaua Beach Park. If you're coming from the south, Papalaua is just under a mile north of the tunnel.

Makena to White Rock

This route has long stretches of paddling, but it's interspersed with some of the best snorkeling on Maui. I start by following the shoreline and rounding the point on the right. This puts me into the Five Caves - Five Graves area. I always plan on skipping this spot and snorkeling it on my way back, but it never seems to work out that way—it's just too nice. There are two underwater ridges that extend from shore here. If you watch the water you'll notice it swirls around them with every falling swell. They're packed with a variety of fish and beautiful coral. Nearer to shore are several underwater arches.

After pulling anchor at Five Caves, I'll drop it again 300 yards north just off Chang's Beach. It's a great little beach found on the south side of the Makena Surf Condos. If you're without an anchor, you can leave your kayak on shore and swim back out to snorkel the reef. It's not a large area, but it's gorgeous and the coral is in excellent shape. Please help keep it that way and watch your fins in tight spots. The reef here extends around the rocky point to Po'olenalena Beach. If one side is murky, the other is often clear. Chang's seems to be a favored cleaning station for the local turtle population, where small fish nibble algae off their shells. If you're lucky enough to come upon a "turtle cleaning," enjoy the moment but give them plenty of space.

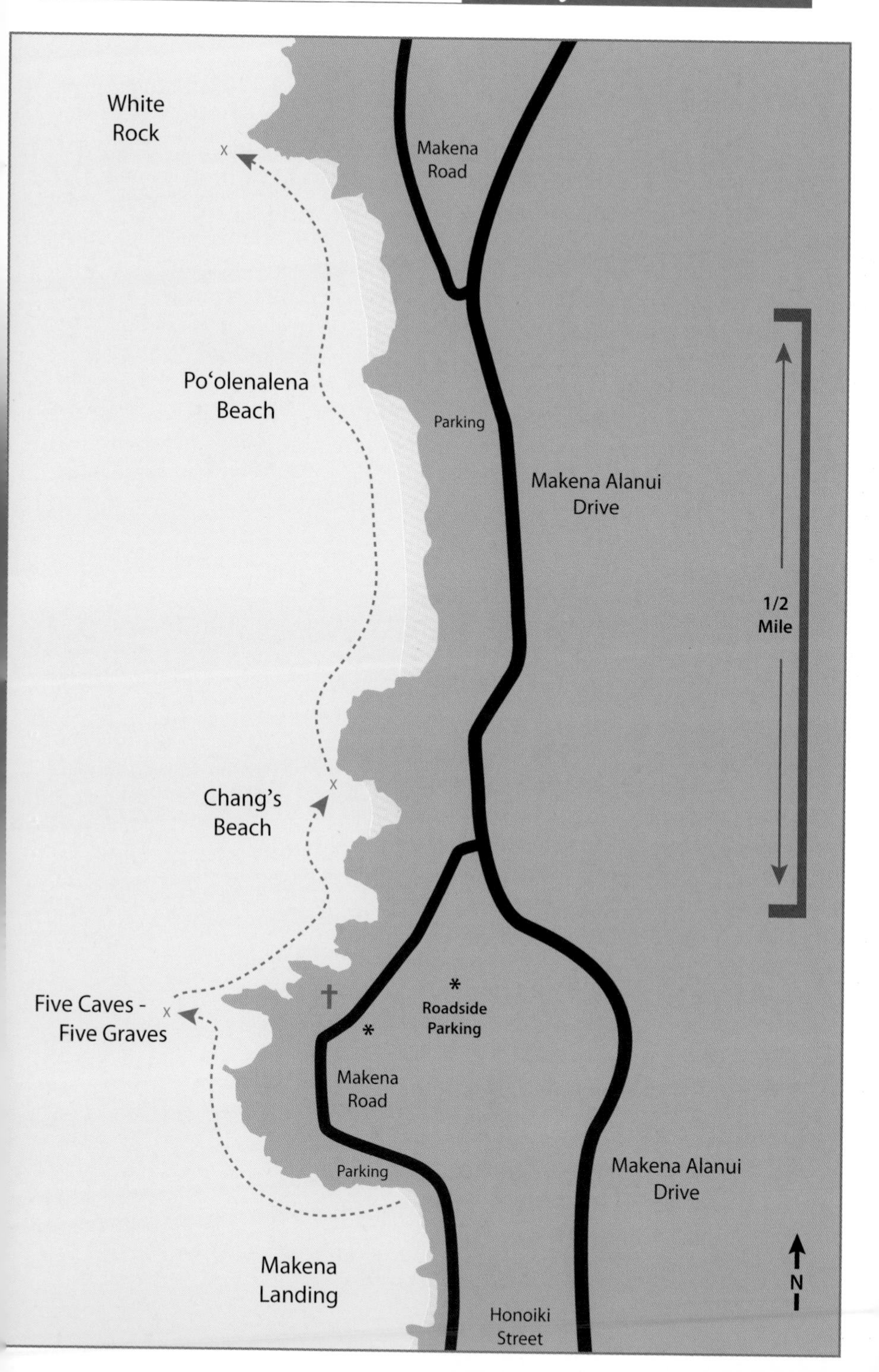
White
Rock
Makena
Road
Po'olenalena
Beach
Parking
Makena Alanui
Drive
1/2
Mile
Chang's
Beach
Five Caves -
Five Graves
Roadside
Parking
Makena
Road
Parking
Makena Alanui
Drive
Makena
Landing
Honoiki
Street
N

The next stop is a half-mile north off the large rocky point with the big oceanfront home above. This area is known as White Rock. It's a long slog, but offers good snorkeling and the attractive backdrop of Po'olenalena Beach. If you want a chuckle, swing near shore toward the north end of the beach. This stretch seems to be popular with the no-tan-lines crowd—though most resemble "George Costanza."

The reef around White Rock encompasses a large area of varying depths. It's punctuated with shelves, deep vertical walls, and shallow areas with large patches of coral just a few feet below the surface. The varied terrain also provides a nice array of sea life. I've encountered everything from a parade of manta rays gliding around a submerged pinnacle to a tiny dragon wrasse working the pebbles at the base of a rock wall. It's also a good spot to find moray eels. I like to explore as much as time and conditions permit, either dropping anchor or towing the kayak behind me. The return trip to Makena Landing is just over a mile.

Distance: Makena Landing to White Rock, 2½ miles round trip.

Facilities: Restrooms and showers at Makena Landing.

Location: South Maui, Makena Road, about 2½ miles south of Wailea.

From Wailea, drive south for 2½ miles on Wailea Alanui Road / Makena Alanui Road. Turn right on Honoiki Road, then right on Makena Road. You'll find Makena Landing just up the road on your left.

Towing a kayak while snorkeling

Makena to Pu'u Ola'i

This kayak excursion is one of my favorite trips. I like to follow the shore-line straight out to the point, swing north, then explore the Five Caves - Five Graves area. There are several spots to drop anchor and explore the underwater ridges that extend from shore. From here, I head south and paddle to the area just past the launch site and offshore of the first group of houses. There's a mass of lava rock that breaks the surface about 80 yards out. The water here is often murky but if it's clear, the snorkeling is awesome with nice patches of coral extending to the point a hundred yards to the south. Lots of turtles and morays can be found through here.

My next stop is the reef at the south end of Maluaka Beach, just past the resort. I usually drop anchor and explore the shallower areas for a while. If you take your time, there are some nice finds. I once spent 40 minutes fascinated by two octopuses hiding on a small coral head. It's amazing to see them change not only their color, but the shape and texture of their skin.

The reef extends another 300 yards south along the shoreline and around the point. I like to snorkel the area towing the kayak behind me. Sea turtles are common and the underwater topography becomes

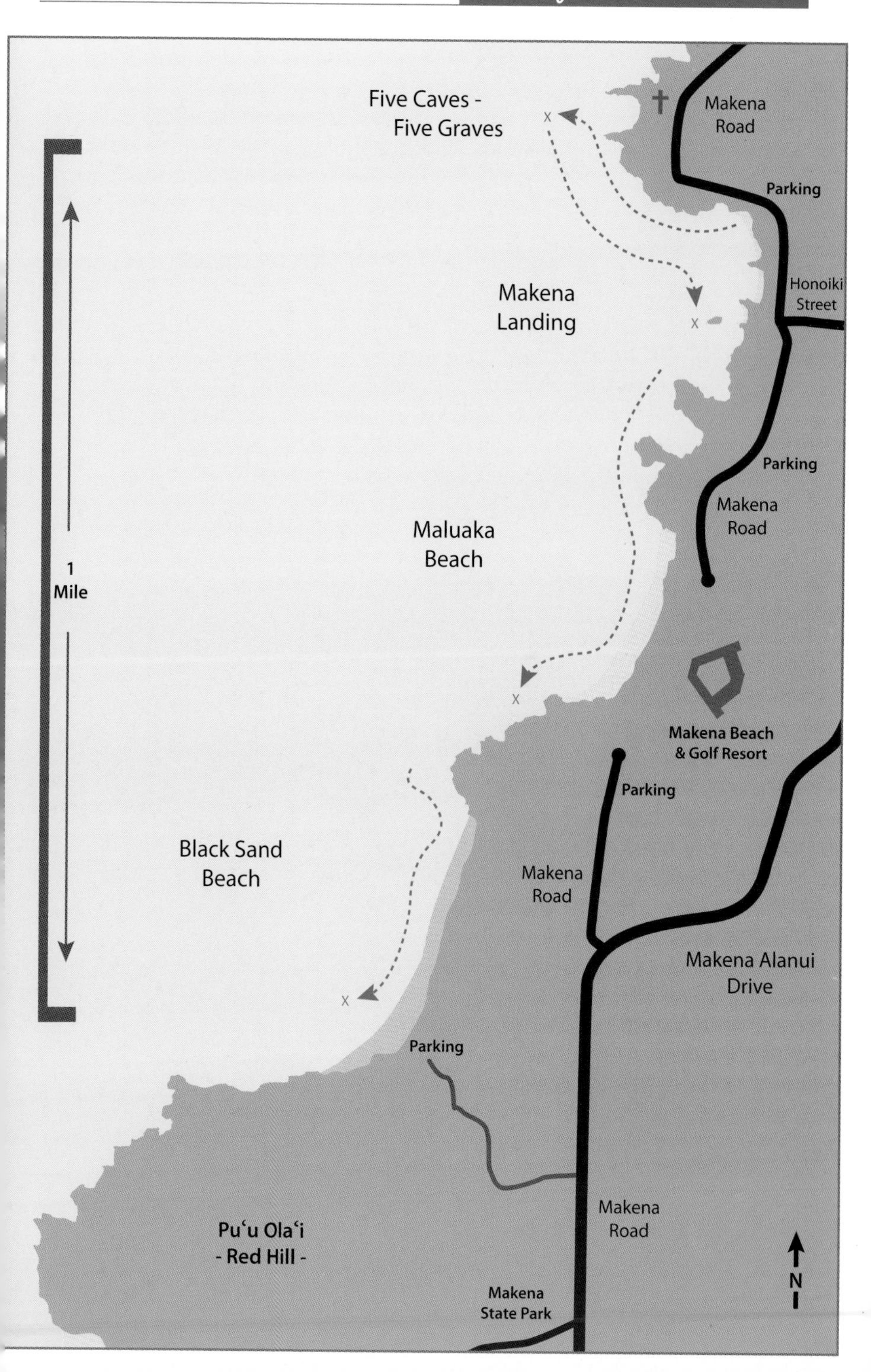

Five Caves -
Five Graves
Makena
Road
Parking
Makena
Landing
Honoiki
Street
Parking
Makena
Road
Maluaka
Beach
1
Mile
Makena Beach
& Golf Resort
Parking
Black Sand
Beach
Makena
Road
Makena Alanui
Drive
Parking
Makena
Road
Pu'u Ola'i
- Red Hill -
Makena
State Park
N

incredible the closer you get to the point. Filled with lava rock arches and numerous crevices, it's a memorable area to snorkel.

Following Maluaka, I paddle the shoreline about 30 yards out and make my way south for another quarter-mile, putting me about three-quarters of the way down Black Sand Beach. When I find a spot with decent clarity, I hit the water and tow the kayak behind me. It's a huge area that extends over a hundred yards from shore and continues in varying depths all the way around Pu'u Ola'i to Little Beach. If you have plenty of time, be sure to snorkel the cliff edges as well as the waters further out. There's an abundance of fish, eels, and large patches of coral. You may also find the remains of a lobster or two, a favored meal of various sharks—yikes! Rational or not, it's sure nice to have your kayak close by. The return trip to Makena Landing is a 1½ mile paddle.

Distance: Makena Landing to Pu'u Ola'i, 3 miles round trip.

Facilities: Restrooms and showers at Makena Landing.

Location: South Maui, Makena Road, about 2½ miles south of Wailea.

From Wailea, drive 2½ miles south on Wailea Alanui Road / Makena Alanui Road. Turn right on Honoiki Road, then right on Makena Road. You'll find Makena Landing Beach Park just up the road on your left.

Kayaking to Pu‘u Ola‘i

Makena Highlights

If you have a limited amount of time but want to see the highlights of the Makena Landing area, this is the route to take. Paddle along the shoreline and round the point to the right. This is the Five Caves - Five Graves area. If you've read the descriptions of the other routes, you'll know to drop anchor anywhere along one of the two underwater ridges. It's great snorkeling with lots of fish. You may also want to venture over to the shoreline rocks, the underwater landscape is really cool with canyons, arches and cave-like pockets.

After exploring Five Caves, paddle north to the reef off Chang's Beach. It's the first sandy beach you'll see and has condominiums on the north side. The snorkeling here extends for 200 yards around the rocks, but the nicest portion is on the south side. Tread lightly. The coral here is in great shape, so please do your part to keep it that way. There's a good variety of fish and it's hard not to see at least one turtle.

The next stop is a half-mile to the south. Paddle back past Five Caves and veer toward shore when Makena Landing comes into view. Near the shoreline and just south of the launch site is a jumble of lava rock breaking the water's surface. It's about 80 yards out. If the clarity looks good, hit the water. It's often cloudy, but holds a treasure when it's clear.

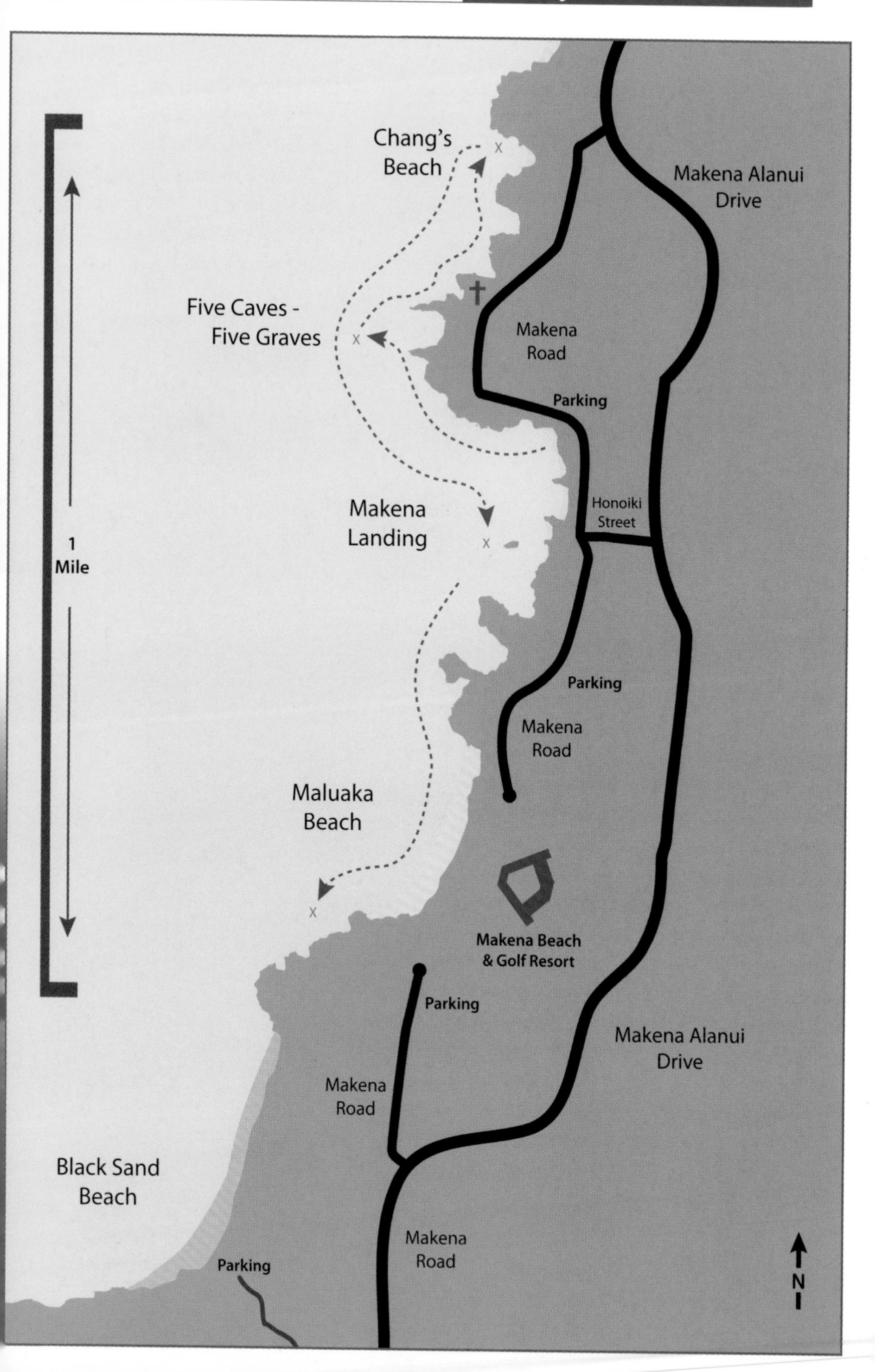
Chang's Beach
Makena Alanui Drive
Five Caves - Five Graves
Makena Road
Parking
Honoiki Street
Makena Landing
1 Mile
Parking
Makena Road
Maluaka Beach
Makena Beach & Golf Resort
Parking
Makena Alanui Drive
Makena Road
Black Sand Beach
Makena Road
Parking
N

Turtles, eels, and exceptional coral abound. You'll find patches with great snorkeling extending south to the rocky point. I usually tow the kayak behind me through this area.

The last section of this route is the reef at Maluaka Beach. It's another half-mile south and worth the trip if you have time. I like to shadow the shoreline then drop anchor after reaching the rocks just off the south side of the beach. The area is huge and stretches 250 yards to the rocky point in the south. There are several underwater crevices and arches, a wide range of fish, eels, and almost always a few turtles. This area is one of the "Turtle Towns" visited by the snorkel boats. Take your time and you might even see an octopus. Despite their best efforts at camouflage I've found several through here.

Distance: 3½ miles round trip.

Facilities: Restrooms and showers at Makena Landing.

Location: South Maui, Makena Road, about 2½ miles south of Wailea.

From Wailea, drive south for 2½ miles on Wailea Alanui Road / Makena Alanui Road. Turn right on Honoiki Road, then right on Makena Road. You'll find Makena Landing Beach Park just up the road on your left.

Red pencil urchins dot the coral reefs near Makena.

How to Say it...

If you're a first time visitor to the Hawaiian islands, learning how to pronounce the names of Maui's beaches, bays, cities, and streets may seem like an impossible task—especially with all those vowels! But the longer you see and hear the language, somehow your brain begins to adjust. This introduction along with a pronunciation guide for the locations mentioned in this book will get you started.

Keep in mind every language has exceptions and is more complicated to learn than what can be covered in a few paragraphs. Other guides may use different phonetic spellings, but hopefully we arrive at similar pronunciation to get you headed in the right direction.

So on to a few basics... There are 13 letters in the Hawaiian alphabet, five vowels: **a e i o u** and eight consonants: **ʻ h k l m n p w**.

Vowels: Hawaiian vowel sounds are a little different from English. Think: "ah, eh, ee, oh, oo." While English vowels have a variety of sounds, Hawaiian vowels are always pronounced the same. Sometimes you'll see vowels with a line over them. This line is called a "kahakō" and indicates the vowel is spoken with a longer duration.

Vowel sounds			With kahakō - longer duration	
a	"ah"	as in saw	ā	"ahh"
e	"eh"	as in red	ē	"ehh"
i	"ee"	as in see	ī	"eee"
o	"oh"	as in so	ō	"ohh"
u	"oo"	as in moo	ū	"ooo"

Consonants: Hawaiian consonants sound similar to English with the exception of **W** which can be spoken with a "v" or "w" sound. When **W** appears after **E** or **I** (and sometimes after **A**, or when **W** *starts* a word) the "v" sound is often used. You've likely heard Hawaiʻi pronounced both ways: "Ha why-ee" and "Ha vye-ee."

There's also a special consonant called an ʻokina that looks like an upside down apostrophe (ʻ). Whenever you see an ʻokina it's telling you to take a short pause, sort of like the break when you say, "oh-oh." An ʻokina is commonly found between two vowels, especially when a vowel is repeated, as in the state's name Hawaiʻi or the surfer beach Ho'okipa. Probably the most ignored 'okina is the one used to spell the popular resort area, Ka'anapali. Often mispronounced, "Kah nuh pa lee," it's really, "Kah 'ah na pa lee." Make a quick pause whenever you see an 'okina and you'll fit right in. Just don't over do it or you'll sound more like a malihini (visitor) trying to sound like a local—sometimes you just can't win!

Unfortunately it's quite common for the kahakō and the 'okina to be left out of writing which can change not only how to say a word but also its meaning. For those unfamiliar with the language this can result in amusing miscommunication. For example, the three letter word "pau" can be interpreted in many ways:

- pau = finished, done
- pa'ū = moist, damp
- pa'u = soot, smudge
- pā'ū = a woman's skirt

Diphthongs: Sometimes vowels work in pairs called diphthongs where two vowels form one sound. Diphthongs complicate things, but are very common in the Hawaiian language so it's important to get to know them. If you could slow down a fluent Hawaiian speaker you could almost hear the sound of each vowel, but they're spoken together so quickly they form ***one sound*** and ***one syllable***.

ae sounds like "ah + eh" similar to the word "eye"
ai sounds like "ah + ee" similar to "eye" as well
ao sounds like "ah + oh" similar to "ow" in cow
au sounds like "ah + oo" similar to "ow" in "Ow! That hurts!"
ei sounds like "eh + ee" similar to "ei" in eight
eu sounds like "eh + oo" similar to the vowels in "hey you"
oi sounds like "oh + ee" similar to "oi" in voice
ou sounds like "oh + oo" similar to "Ohhh!" or "owe"

You'll notice some diphthongs have very similar sounds. To hear the subtle difference, pronounce each vowel separately, then increase your speed until you hear ***one*** sound. The "similar to" suggestions are close. "Ai" and "au" are very common, get to know them first.

A few other tips...

- All Hawaiian words end in a vowel, so do all syllables.
- Syllables are short! They can only include: a consonant + one or two vowels (a diphthong), **OR** a single vowel or a diphthong.

Common Words & Place Names

aloha	(ah lo ha)	greeting, hello, goodbye, love
mahalo	(mah ha lo)	thank you
ʻono	(oh no)	delicious
pono	(po no)	excellent
kapu	(kah poo)	forbidden, keep out, sacred

People

kāne	(kah neh)	man/ husband
wahine	(wah/vah hee neh)	woman/ wife
keiki	(kay kee)	children
kupuna	(koo poo nah)	grandparent or ancestor
ʻohana	(oh ha nah)	family, relatives
malihini	(mah lee hee nee)	visitor
kamaʻāina	(kah mah-eye nah)	resident, not a visitor

Outdoors

pali	(pah lee)	cliff
ʻaʻā	(ah-ahh)	sharp lava rock
makai	(mah kye)	toward the sea
mauka	(mow kah)	toward the mountain
mauna	(mow nah)	mountain
ʻāina	(eye nah)	land, sacred or native lands
kiawe	(kee ah veh)	thorny mesquite trees
pua	(poo ah)	flower
hale	(ha leh)	house or building
lānai	(lah nye)	porch patio

Ocean

kai	(kye)	seaside, sea
moana	(mo ah nah)	ocean
one	(oh neh)	sand
honu	(ho noo)	turtle
iʻa	(ee-ah)	fish
manō	(mah no)	shark
kohola	(ko ho lah)	whale
puhi	(poo hee)	eel
heʻe	(heh-eh)	octopus
mūheʻe	(moo heh-eh)	squid
ula	(oo lah)	lobster

Hawaiian Islands (heading west)

Hawai'i	(Ha why-ee **or** Ha vye-ee)
Maui	(Mow ee)
Kaho'olawe	(Kah ho-oh lah veh)
Moloka'i	(Mo lo kah-ee)
Lāna'i	(Lah nah-ee)
O'ahu	(Oh-ah hoo)
Kaua'i	(Kow wah-ee)
Ni'ihau	(Nee-ee how)

Highways

Honoapi'ilani Hwy (30)	(Ho no ah pee-ee lah nee)
Kūihelani Hwy (380)	(Koo ee heh lah nee)
Mokulele Hwy (311)	(Mo koo leh leh)
Pi'ilani Hwy (31)	(Pee-ee lah nee)
Hāna Hwy (36)	(Hah nah)
Haleakalā Hwy (37)	(Hah leh ah kah la)

West Maui Locations (north to south)

Kapalua	(Kah pah loo ah)
Nāpili	(Nah pee lee)
Kahana	(Kah ha nah)
Honokōwai	(Ho no ko why)
Kā'anapali	(Kah-ah nah pa lee)
Lahaina	(Lah hye nah)
Olowalu	(Oh lo wah loo)
Ukumehame	(Oo koo meh ha meh)

Beaches and Bays

Honolua Bay	(Ho no loo ah)
Mokule'ia Bay	(Mo koo leh ee ah)
Oneloa Beach	(Oh neh lo ah)
Nāmalu Bay	(Nah mah loo)
Kahekili Beach	(Kah heh kee lee)
Launiupoko Beach	(L+"ow" nee oo po ko)
Pāpalaua Beach	(Pa pa l+"ow" ah)

Streets

Hui Drive	(Hoo ee)
Hale Ali'i	(Hah leh Ah lee-ee)
Nāpilihau Street	(Nah pee lee how)

South Maui Locations	(north to south)
Kihei	(Kee hay)
Wailea	(Why leh ah)
Mākena	(Mah keh nah)

Beaches and Bays	
Kalama Beach	(Kah la ma)
Kama'ole Beach	(Kah mah-oh leh)
Keawakapu Beach	(Keh ah vah kah poo)
Mōkapu Beach	(Mo kah poo)
Ulua Beach	(Oo loo ah)
Palauea Beach	(Pa l+"ow" eh ah)
Po'olenalena Beach	(Po-oh leh nah leh nah)
Maluaka Beach	(Mah loo ah kah)
Ahihi Bay	(Ah hee hee)

South Maui Sites and Streets	
Molokini Crater	(Mo lo kee nee)
Pu'u Ōla'i	(Poo-oo Oh lah-ee) Maui's big red hill
Alanui Keali'i Drive	(Ah lah noo ee Keh ah lee ee)
Keonekai Road	(Keh oh neh kye)
Honoiki Street	(Ho no ee kee)
Kaukahi Street	(Kow ka hee)
Kilohana Drive	(Kee lo ha nah)
Okolani Drive	(Oh ko lah nee)
Pi'ikea Avenue	(Pee-ee keh ah)
Wailea Iki	(Why leh ah Ee kee)

Central Maui Locations	
Mā'alaea	(Mah-ah lye ah)
Wailuku	(Why loo koo)
Kahului	(Kah hoo loo ee)
Pu'unēnē	(Poo-oo neh neh)
'Īao Valley	(EE ow) similar to meow without the "m"

Up Country Locations	
Makawao	(Mah kah wow)
Pukalani	(Poo kah lah nee)
Kula	(Koo lah)
Haleakalā	(Hah leh ah kah la)

Ke'anae Peninsula

Heading to Hāna

Pā'ia	(Pah-ee ah)
Ho'okipa Beach	(Ho-oh kee pah)
Ha'ikū	(Hah-ee koo)
Huelo	(Hoo eh lo)
Honomanū Bay	(Ho no mah noo)
Ke'anae	(Keh-ah nye)
Wailua	(Why loo ah)
Nāhiku	(Nah hee koo)
Wai'ānapanapa	(Why-ah nah pah nah pah) State Park
Hāna	(Hah nah)
Hāmoa Beach	(Hah mo ah)
Kīpahulu	(Kee pah hoo loo)
'Ohe'o Gulch	(Oh heh-oh)
Kaupō	(Kow po)

Index

Whitemouth Moray – In Watercolor

For more images of the beautiful island of Maui,
please visit:

senseofplacemaui.com